Thinking and Writing about Psychology

to accompany

Psychology: The Core

Spencer A. Rathus
Montclair State University

THOMSON

WADSWORTH

Australia • Canada • Mexico • Singapore • Spain • United Kingdom • United States

ISBN: 0-15-507460-1

Wadsworth Group/Thomson Learning
10 Davis Drive
Belmont CA 94002-3098
USA

For information about our products, contact us:
Thomson Learning Academic Resource Center
1-800-423-0563
http://www.wadsworth.com

For permission to use material from this text, contact us by
Web: http://www.thomsonrights.com
Fax: 1-800-730-2215
Phone: 1-800-730-2214

Printed in the United States of America
10 9 8 7 6 5 4 3

THINKING AND WRITING ABOUT PSYCHOLOGY   1

THINKING AND WRITING EXERCISES   34

1
THINKING AND WRITING ABOUT PSYCHOLOGY

This book is primarily intended to stimulate students to think and write about psychology. In doing so, this book will also help colleges, professors, and students to meet two widespread pedagogical objectives:

1. Critical thinking
2. Writing across the curriculum

The emphasis on critical thinking is consistent with guidelines suggested by the Association of American Colleges and by the American Psychological Association.

GOALS FOR AN UNDERGRADUATE EDUCATION IN PSYCHOLOGY

Psychologists are working with the Association of American Colleges to establish goals and guidelines for undergraduate education. A psychology task force listed several goals for an undergraduate education in psychology (McGovern, 1989). The first goal was to foster a "knowledge base" consisting of important "theories, research findings, and issues in psychology." The second goal was to promote skills in "critical thinking and reasoning." These thinking skills involve the following:

- Development of skepticism about explanations and conclusions
- The ability to inquire about causes and effects
- Refinement of curiosity about behavior
- Knowledge of research methods
- The ability to critically analyze arguments

The focus on critical thinking reflects the widespread belief that a college education is intended to do more than provide you with a data bank of useful knowledge. That is, it is also meant to provide you with intellectual tools that allow you to learn from and analyze information independently. With these tools, you can continue to educate yourself throughout your life.

Colleges nurture academic freedom, thus few professors require (or want) students to share and express their own beliefs. Overall, professors are more concerned that students learn how to question and critically examine psychological theory and research, the points of view of other people, and even their own convictions and values. This does not mean that professors insist that students change their beliefs, either. It does mean, however, that professors usually ask students to *support* the views that they express in class and in their writing. If students' definitions of terms are unclear, if their premises are shaky, or if their arguments are illogical, professors may encourage other students to challenge them or may personally point out the fallacies in their arguments. Most professors want students to learn to recognize the premises of their arguments, to consider whether they really accept these premises, and to understand whether they draw logical conclusions from them. The following section more deeply examines the issue of critical thinking.

CRITICAL THINKING

The object of education is to prepare the young to educate themselves throughout their lives.

—ROBERT M. HUTCHINS

A great many people think they are thinking when they are merely rearranging their prejudices.

—WILLIAM JAMES

Most people take a certain number of "truths" for granted. One such truth is that authority figures such as doctors and government leaders usually provide us with factual information and are generally equipped to make the decisions that affect our lives (Kimble, 1994; Murray, 1997). However, when two doctors disagree as to whether surgery is necessary to cure an illness, how can both be correct? When political leaders who all claim to have the "best interests" of the nation at heart fling accusations and epithets at one another, how can we know whom to trust? If we are to be conscientious, productive citizens of the nation and the world, we need to seek pertinent information to make our own decisions and rely on our analytical abilities to judge its accuracy. This book will help you learn how to seek and analyze information that lies within the province of psychology, but the critical thinking skills you acquire can be applied in all of your courses and other adult undertakings.

In the fifteenth century, it was widely believed that the earth was flat. In the sixteenth century, it was widely believed that the sun revolved around the earth. It seems that widely held beliefs are invariably replaced by others in the fullness of time. It is the hallmark of an educated person to remain skeptical of accepted views and to regard even the most popular beliefs as working assumptions. In the twentieth century, most astronomers widely believe that the universe began with a "big bang" and has been expanding ever since that event occurred. It is fascinating to speculate on what views will replace these beliefs in the future.

To help students evaluate claims, arguments, and widely held beliefs, most colleges today encourage *critical thinking*. Critical thinking has many meanings. On one level, it means taking nothing for granted. It means not believing information just because it is in print or was put forth by authority figures or celebrities. It means not necessarily believing that it is healthful to express all your feelings, even if a friend in analysis urges you to do so. On another level, critical thinking refers to a process of thoughtfully analyzing and probing the questions, statements, and arguments of others. It means examining definitions of terms and the premises or assumptions behind arguments, and then scrutinizing the logic with which arguments are developed.

Principles of Critical Thinking

Let us consider some principles of critical thinking:

1. *Be skeptical.* Keep an open mind. Politicians and advertisers try to persuade you. Even research reported in the media or in textbooks may take a certain slant. Extend this principle to yourself. If you examine the information critically, you might discover that some of your own attitudes and beliefs are superficial or unfounded. Accept nothing as true until you have examined the evidence.

2. *Examine definitions of terms.* Some statements are true when a term is defined in one way but not when it is defined in another way. Consider the statement "Head Start programs have raised children's IQs." The correctness of the statement depends on the definition of "IQ." (Your text explains that *IQ* has a specific meaning and is not exactly the same as *intelligence*.)

3. *Examine the assumptions or premises of arguments.* Consider the statement: "We cannot learn about humans by engaging in research with animals." One premise in the statement seems to be that humans are not animals. However, we are animals. (Would you rather be a plant?)

4. *Be cautious in drawing conclusions from evidence.* For many years, studies showed that most clients who receive psychotherapy improve. It was therefore generally assumed that psychotherapy worked. However, in the late 1950s a psychologist named Hans Eysenck pointed out that most psychologically troubled people who did *not* receive psychotherapy also improved. The question thus becomes whether people receiving psychotherapy are *more* likely to improve than those who do not receive psychotherapy are. Thus, research on the effectiveness of psychotherapy carefully compares the benefits of therapy techniques with the benefits of other techniques or of no treatment at all. Be skeptical, moreover, when a friend swears by the effectiveness of megavitamin therapy for colds. What is the nature of the "evidence"? Is it convincing?

   Correlational evidence is also inferior to experimental evidence as a way of determining cause and effect. Consider the statement, "Alcohol causes aggression," in the following principle.

5. *Consider alternative interpretations of research evidence.* Does alcohol cause aggression? Is the assertion that it does so truth or fiction? Evidence certainly shows a clear *connection,* or "correlation," between alcohol and aggression. That is, many people who commit violent crimes have been drinking. However, does the evidence show that this connection is *causal*? Consider the differences between the correlational and experimental methods as you think about your answer.

6. *Do not oversimplify.* Most human behavior involves interactions of genetic and environmental influences. Also consider the issue of whether psychotherapy helps people with psychological problems. A broad answer to this question—a simple yes or no—might be oversimplifying. It is more worthwhile to ask, "What *type* of psychotherapy, practiced by *whom,* is most helpful for *what kind of problem*?"

7. *Do not overgeneralize.* Consider the statement that you cannot learn about humans by engaging in research with animals. Is the truth of the matter an all-or-nothing issue? Are there certain kinds of information that we can obtain about people from research with animals? What kinds of things are you likely to be able to learn only through research with people?

8. *Apply critical thinking to all areas of life.* A skeptical attitude and a demand for evidence are not simply useful skills while you are in college. They are of value in all areas of life. Be skeptical when you are bombarded by television commercials, when political causes try to sweep you up, or when you see the latest cover stories about Elvis and UFOs in the supermarket tabloids. How many times have you heard the claim "Studies have shown that . . ."? Perhaps such claims seem convincing, but ask yourself the following: Who ran the studies? Were the researchers neutral scientists, or were they biased toward obtaining certain results?

As noted by the educator Robert M. Hutchins, "The object of education is to prepare the young to educate themselves throughout their lives." One of the primary ways of educating yourself is through critical thinking.

Common Errors in Arguments

Another aspect of critical thinking is learning to recognize the errors in other people's claims and arguments. Consider the following examples:

1. Arguments directed to the person. The views of Sigmund Freud, the founder of psychodynamic theory, were assaulted almost as soon as they were publicized, both by members of his circle, such as Carl Jung, and by psychologists of other schools, such as behaviorists. Freud has been alternately referred to as an ingenious, compassionate scientist and as an elitist faker who based his theories on the fantasy lives of bored, wealthy women. Freud's personality and motives may be of historic interest, but they do not affect the accuracy of his views. Theories should be judged on the evidence, not on the character of the theorist.

2. Appeals to force. In the seventeenth century, Galileo invented the telescope and discovered that the earth revolved around the sun, rather than vice versa. The Catholic Church, however, taught that the earth was at the center of the universe. Galileo was condemned for heresy and warned that he would be burned at the stake if he did not confess the error of his ways. Galileo apparently agreed with Shakespeare that "the better part of valor is discretion" and retracted his views. But the facts are what they are. Social approval or threats of violence do not make arguments correct or incorrect.

3. Appeals to authority. You have probably often heard arguments such as this one: "Well, my mother/teacher/minister says this is true, and I think that he/she knows more about it than you do." Appeals to authority can be persuasive or infuriating, depending on whether you agree with them. However, it matters not *who* makes an assertion—even if that person is a psychological celebrity such as Sigmund Freud, William James, or John B. Watson. An argument is true or false on its own merits. Consider the evidence presented in arguments, not the person making the argument, no matter how exalted.

4. Appeals to popularity. The appeal to popularity is cousin to the appeal to authority. The people making the pitches in television commercials are usually very popular—either because they are good looking or because they are celebrities. Again, evaluate the evidence being presented and ignore the appeal of the person making the pitch.

The argument that you should do or believe something because "everyone is doing it" is another type of appeal to popularity—one that gets many people involved in activities they later regret.

In sum, be skeptical and examine evidence critically. Acquiring an education means more than memorizing information and learning how to solve chemistry and math problems. It also means acquiring the tools to think critically so that you can continue to educate yourself throughout your life.

As you complete the writing exercises in this book, be skeptical of claims and arguments. Critically examine the evidence presented rather than focusing on the authority, force, or appeal of the people making the argument.

Let us assume that you will become a more critical thinker. Let us now see how you can express your thoughts in writing. There is no doubt that writing comes more easily to some people than to others. However, we all can profit from attending to a few principles about writing. Writing skills, similar to critical thinking skills, will serve us well for the rest of our lives.

WRITING ACROSS THE CURRICULUM

Books are the carriers of civilization.

—BARBARA TUCHMAN

No man but a blockhead ever wrote except for money.

—SAMUEL JOHNSON

I love being a writer. What I can't stand is the paperwork.

—PETER DE VRIES

Writing is the only thing that, when I do it, I don't feel I should be doing something else.

—GLORIA STEINEM

"Writing across the curriculum" refers to writing in every subject. You naturally write in an English composition course, and you may be assigned brief or long papers in many other courses. The concept behind writing across the curriculum is that every subject presents an opportunity for expressing yourself in writing and enhancing your writing skills.

Why all this emphasis on writing? Throughout high school and college, many students have the feeling that compositions and papers are little more than part of the price they have to pay to get a diploma and, eventually, a decent job. They do not see writing as something that is valuable in itself.

The fact is that writing is essential, not only in college but also in most professional careers. Business executives need to be able to communicate their ideas through writing. Marketing plans, advertising copy, and proposals for new products must all be fleshed out in words and sentences. Very few lawyers put on courtroom shows such as the fabled Perry Mason; most lawyers spend far more time writing contracts and persuasive letters. Technicians, engineers, and scientists have to be able to write precise reports. Think of all the writing that goes into directions for using a stove or setting up a personal computer. Consider the detailed writing that is found in armed forces weapons manuals. Engineers and scientists also write technical articles for journals; they review the research in their fields and report on their own research studies. They have to be able to write clearly enough so that other people can follow their directions and arrive at the same results accurately and safely. Doctors, psychologists, counselors, nurses, and dental hygienists must be able to write reports describing the problems and progress of their patients and clients. Managers of fast-food restaurants write evaluations of employees. Everyone writes business letters of one kind or another—or is inconvenienced if he or she cannot.

It may seem to you that thinking precedes writing. That is, you have to have something to write *about*. But learning how to write also helps to teach you how to *think*. Part of writing certainly involves proper spelling and usage. In writing, however, you are also forced to organize your ideas and present them logically. Training and practice in writing are therefore also training and practice in thinking.

Writing skills are thus not for college only. Writing skills are not just the province of English teachers, poets, novelists, and journalists. They are for everyone who is receiving an education and contemplating a career.

Many college students fear writing assignments because they did not receive enough training in high school to make them comfortable with writing. Most college writing instructors view their job as enhancing their students' creativity, critical thinking, and explanatory powers, not as teaching students basic sentence structure and punctuation. Professors in other disciplines often rely completely on short-answer tests to arrive at grades. (They may protest that their job is to teach their subject, not to suffer through their students' incoherent essays and papers.) High school English teachers sometimes complain that basic skills were not taught in the elementary schools. Elementary school teachers, in turn, often criticize children's home environments for not helping to incubate basic writing skills. Writing skills, in short, are valued in college and are essential afterward but are taught only by a minority of instructors in a few disciplines.

Kinds of Writing

There are many kinds of writing. Writing can be broken down into fiction (imaginary happenings such as short stories, plays, and novels) and nonfiction (such as directions for assembling machines, essays, theme papers, and term papers). Fiction writing is usually taught in creative writing courses, although it is sometimes assigned in freshman composition classes. Students do not need to be good at writing fiction to get by in college, unless they are making up excuses as to why they are late with their assignments! Overall, however, college students are required to show or develop some skill at writing nonfiction.

The kinds of nonfiction required of college students are mostly essay answers on tests, theme papers, and term papers. Here we focus on theme papers and research papers, some of which are term papers. A theme is a relatively short paper and is the most common type of paper assigned in courses such as freshman composition. There are different kinds of themes, including argumentative, descriptive, and expository.

ARGUMENTATIVE THEME The aim of the *argumentative theme* is to persuade the reader to adopt a certain point of view. Papers intended to convince the reader that Lady Macbeth was motivated by infertility or that the greenhouse effect will eventually cause persistent droughts in the midwestern breadbasket are argumentative.

DESCRIPTIVE THEME A *descriptive theme* paints persons, places, or ideas in words. The infamous "What I Did on My Summer Vacation" theme is basically descriptive. If you have poetic urges, it is usually best to give vent to them in descriptive themes. Expository themes are explanatory in nature. They are concrete and logically developed.

EXPOSITORY THEME *Expository themes* apply to the instructions in your cookbook for concocting guacamole and to laboratory reports. Each discipline (e.g., art, biology, physics, psychology) has its own way of doing things and its own traditions, but they also have some things in common. For example, explanations are kept as brief and precise as possible. Usually you explain what you set out to do, why you set out to do it, what you actually did, what you found out, and, sometimes, the implications of what you discovered.

TYPES OF PSYCHOLOGY PAPERS

The types of papers or articles that are printed in psychology journals are examples of expository themes. Three of the most common kinds of expository themes found in the psychological literature are reports of empirical research studies, reviews of the literature on various topics, and theoretical articles.

These papers are most often written in the "American Psychological Association (APA) format." This format is the standard for articles that are published in APA journals. Most psychology journals that are not published by the APA also require the APA format.

The APA format is somewhat rigid, but its purpose is to help writers report information clearly and concisely, so that readers may present the information without obstacles. Put another way: The APA format is designed to prevent writers from "getting in the way" of reporting their research findings or theoretical concepts.

Reports of Empirical Studies

Empirical studies are reports of original research. Such reports must be "to the point" (show economy in expression) and must be broken into standard sections. The usual sections or parts of reports of empirical research studies are as follows:

- *Introduction* The introduction sets the stage for your research by stating the problem, briefly reviewing previous research in the area, and showing how your research will test or answer some of the issues in the area.
- *Method* This section explains what you did so clearly that people reading the report could replicate (duplicate) your work. Describe the subjects or participants, how they were selected for the study, how many actually participated, and how many withdrew throughout the course of the study; the procedures that were used, including the treatments and the equipment; and the methods of assessment that were employed to measure the dependent variables (outcomes). If the details of the treatment or the apparatus are lengthy, you may include them in an appendix at the end of the article or indicate, in a footnote, how the reader may obtain more detailed information.
- *Results* This section reports your findings.
- *Discussion* The discussion usually begins with a brief summary of the previous three sections (preferably one paragraph). The section then relates the findings to previous research in the area, discusses the implications of the findings for psychological theory, and may suggest directions for future research.

Reviews of the Literature

Rather than report your own original research, literature reviews critically evaluate the previous research in a field of study, summarize what is known for the reader, and point out the strengths and shortcomings of prior research. Psychology textbooks, such as your introductory psychology textbook, may be considered reviews of the literature in various fields of psychology.

Literature reviews frequently summarize research chronologically—that is, they may be organized according to the sequence of the research in the field and show how new ideas developed from the testing of older ideas. They may also be organized topically. One section, for example, may review research with humans, and another section may review studies with lower animals. Another section may review correlational studies, and still another, experimental research. Review articles also have introductions and discussion sections.

Theoretical Papers

Theoretical papers evaluate and advance psychological theory in the fields of psychology. For example, in an introductory section, the author usually states the theoretical problem and summarizes much of the theoretical thinking to the present day. There may then be a discussion of the shortcomings of current theoretical knowledge. Such shortcomings may involve theoretical contradictions or defects.

It may be pointed out, for example, that some tenets of psychodynamic theory are unscientific because they cannot be *disproved*. In addition, it may be shown that the behavior therapy technique of systematic desensitization is not perfectly behavioral because it relies on mental imagery. Other shortcomings may involve inconsistencies between psychological theory and empirical evidence. The evidence, that is, may contradict the theory. The theory may suggest that increasing motivation enhances performance, whereas the evidence may show that increasing motivation helps to a certain point but then impairs performance. In a theoretical article, the concluding sections often suggest modifications to the theory that render it more logical or more consistent with empirical evidence.

Common Features

Psychology articles also include title pages, abstracts, and references. Your instructor may require that assigned papers also contain these elements and that they be written in "APA format."

- *Title Page* The title page should include the following:

  1. Title of the paper. Keep the title as short as possible. The *Publication Manual* of the American Psychological Association (4th ed.; APA, 1994) suggests that phrases such as "A Study of" and "An Experimental Investigation of" are best if omitted from the title.

  2. By-line. The by-line consists of the author's name (or authors' names) and the institution at which the study was conducted (in your case, your college or university).

- *Abstract* Abstracts are used by abstracting and information services to allow scientists who are searching the literature to determine whether your article is among the literature they need to review. When writing an abstract, ask yourself whether the information you are including would allow another individual to make such a decision.

- *References* Psychological articles contain only the works that are cited in the article. They are not the same as a *bibliography,* which may contain a list of all the works on a subject (good luck!) or at least a list of all the works that have had an influence on your writing of the article.

The *Publication Manual* of the American Psychological Association (4th ed.; APA, 1994) notes the following rules for referencing:

1. The text of the paper and the list of references must be in agreement. Every study and author in the paper must be referenced in the list, and vice versa.

2. References are placed in alphabetical order.

3. References to the same authorship are presented chronologically, with the earliest publications listed first.

4. References in the text of the paper and in the reference list are written as shown in Table 1. Figure 1 shows a partial list of references for a psychology article or paper as they would appear at the end of the article or paper.

Term Papers

Term papers differ from briefer theme papers mainly in length. A term paper is named such because the paper should take a good part of the term to write or because the paper is intended to reflect what you have learned during the term. A term paper in psychology is more likely to be a review of the literature on a subject than to be a report of empirical research.

GUIDELINES FOR GOOD WRITING

Just as no two people are exactly alike (even identical twins have their own private thoughts), no two people write exactly alike. Good writing takes many forms. Some people use slang very well; others fare better when they take a more formal approach. Some writers show strong organizational skills; others have a fine poetic touch and the ability to create vivid images through words. Yet, there are a number of guidelines that hold true for most of us the majority of the time.

Complete the Assignment

It may not matter how your intelligence and sophistication shine through or how your prose sparkles if you do not follow instructions and carry out the assignment. Make sure that you understand the instructions. If your professor asks for a reaction paper to an essay, make sure that you understand what the professor means by *reaction paper*. Do not hesitate to ask in class; if you are unclear about how to carry out the assignment, other students may also be confused. If, however, you are concerned that you might take up too much class time, or if you want still more information than can be covered in class, visit your instructor during office hours.

If a general discussion of the requirements does not create a clear picture for you, ask for examples. You can also ask the instructor to show you one or more models (pieces of writing) that fulfill the assignment.

Write for Your Audience

If you are writing a children's story, keep the vocabulary simple and the sentences short. If you are writing an argumentative theme to persuade pro-choice advocates that abortion is morally wrong, do not begin with, "Abortion is murder and people who support abortion are murderers." Such a statement will only serve to alienate your audience. Instead, write a sentence similar to the following, "Abortion is a

TABLE 1

EXAMPLES OF REFERENCES IN APA FORMAT

REFERENCE IN TEXT	REFERENCE IN LIST OF REFERENCES
First citation for two to five authors: (Abramson, Garbed, & Seligman, 1980) Subsequent citations for three or more authors: (Abramson et al., 1980)	Abramson, L. Y., Garbed, J., & Seligman, M. E. P. (1980). Learned helplessness in humans: An attributional hypothesis. In G. Garbed & M. E. P. Seligman (Eds.), *Human helplessness: Theory and application* (pp. 3–34). New York: Academic Press. (Comments: Authors' names are inverted; only initial word [and word following colon] of title of book or chapter of book is capitalized; editors' names are *not* inverted; name of book is underlined [or italicized].)
First and subsequent citations for two book chapter authors: (Agras & Kirkley, 1986)	Agras, W. S., & Kirkley, B. G. (1986). Bulimia: Theories of etiology. In K. D. Brownell & J. P. Foreyt (Eds.), *Handbook of eating disorders* (pp. 367–378). New York: Basic Books.
First and subsequent citations for two journal article authors: (Ainsworth & Bowlby, 1991)	Ainsworth, M. D. S., & Bowlby, J. (1991). An ethological approach to personality development. *American Psychologist, 46,* 333–341. (Comments: Only initial word of journal article or newspaper *article* is capitalized; name of journal is capitalized and underlined [or italicized]; volume of journal is underlined [or italicized]; page numbers stand alone [without "p." or "pp."].)
First and subsequent citations for one author: (Gorman, 1997)	Gorman, J. (1997, April 29). Consciousness studies: From stream to flood. *The New York Times,* pp. C1, C5. (Comments: Newspaper article shows precise date; name of newspaper is capitalized and underlined [or italicized]; no volume or issue number is used; page[s] of article is/are preceded by "p." or "pp.")
Citations for organization as author: (American Psychological Association, 1990)	American Psychological Association. (1990). Ethical principles of psychologists. *American Psychologist, 45,* 390–395.
First and subsequent citations for six or more authors: (Hakim et al., 1998)	Listing for six or more authors: Hakim, A. A., et al. (1998). Effects of walking on mortality among nonsmoking retired men. *New England Journal of Medicine, 338,* 94–99.
First and subsequent citations for single author: (Bandura, 1991)	Bandura, A. (1991). Human agency: The rhetoric and the reality. *The American Psychologist, 46,* 157–162.
Citation for first article by same authorship in given year: (Baron, 1990a)	Baron, R. A. (1990a). Environmentally induced positive affect: Its impact on self-efficacy, task performance, negotiation, and conflict. *Journal of Applied Social Psychology, 20,* 368–384. (Comment: Letter *a* is used to denote reference to first article by the author[s] in a given year.)
Citation for second article by same authorship in given year: (Baron, 1990b)	Baron, R. A. (1990b). Countering the effects of destructive criticism: The relative efficacy of four interventions. *Journal of Applied Psychology, 75,* 235–245. (Comment: Letter *b* is used to denote reference to second article by the author[s] in a given year.)
First citation for five or fewer authors: (Beck, Brown, Berchick, Stewart, & Steer, 1990) Subsequent citations for three or more authors: (Beck et al., 1990) First and subsequent citations for two authors: (Beck & Freeman, 1990)	Beck, A. T., Brown, G., Berchick, R. J., Stewart, B. L., & Steer, R. A. (1990). Relationship between hopelessness and ultimate suicide. *American Journal of Psychiatry, 147,* 190–195.
(Beck & Young, 1985)	Beck, A. T., & Freeman, A. (1990). *Cognitive therapy of personality disorders.* New York: Guilford. (Comment: Book title is underlined or italicized; only first word of title is capitalized.)
(Behrens, 1990)	Beck, A. T., & Young, J. E. (1985). Depression. In D. H. Barlow (Ed.), *Clinical handbook of psychological disorders* (pp. 206–244). New York: Guilford Press. (Comment: Reference to a chapter in a book edited by one editor.)
(Blakeslee, 1992a)	Behrens, D. (1990, September 21). Test-tube baby in tug-of-war. *New York Newsday,* pp. 3, 23. (Comment: Reference to newspaper article found on nonconsecutive pages.)
(Blakeslee, 1992b)	Blakeslee, S. (1992a, January 7). Scientists unraveling chemistry of dreams. *The New York Times,* pp. C1, C10. (Comment: Why is the date listed as 1992a?)
	Blakeslee, S. (1992b, January 22). An epidemic of genital warts raises concern but not alarm. *The New York Times,* p. C12.

FIGURE 1
A partial list of references written in APA format.

References

Abraham, L. K. (1993). *Mama might be better off dead: The failure of health care in urban America.* Chicago: University of Chicago Press.

Abramson, L. Y., Garbed, J., & Seligman, M. E. P. (1980). Learned helplessness in humans: An attributional hypothesis. In G. Garbed & M. E. P. Seligman (Eds.), *Human helplessness: Theory and application* (pp. 3–34). New York: Academic Press.

Ader, D. N., & Johnson, S. B. (1994). Sample description, reporting, and analysis of sex in psychological research: A look at APA and APA division journals in 1990. *American Psychologist, 49,* 216–218.

Agras, W. S., & Kirkley, B. G. (1986). Bulimia: Theories of etiology. In K. D. Brownell & J. P. Foreyt (Eds.), *Handbook of eating disorders* (pp. 367–378). New York: Basic Books.

Ainsworth, M. D. S., & Bowlby, J. (1991). An ethological approach to personality development. *American Psychologist, 46,* 333–341.

Aldag, R. J., & Fuller, S. R. (1993). Beyond fiasco: A reappraisal of the groupthink phenomenon and a new model of group decision processes. *Psychological Bulletin, 113,* 533–552.

Altman, L. K. (1991, June 18). W.H.O. says 40 million will be infected with AIDS virus by 2000. *The New York Times,* p. C3.

American Psychological Association. (1990). Ethical principles of psychologists. *American Psychologist, 45,* 390–395.

Antoni, M. H., et al. (1991). Cognitive-behavioral stress management intervention buffers distress responses and immunologic changes following notification of HIV-1 seropositivity. *Journal of Consulting and Clinical Psychology, 59,* 906–915.

Azar, B. (1999). New pieces filling in addiction puzzle. *APA Monitor, 30*(1), 1, 15.

Baron, R. A. (1990a). Environmentally induced positive affect: Its impact on self-efficacy, task performance, negotiation, and conflict. *Journal of Applied Social Psychology, 20,* 368–384.

Baron, R. A. (1990b). Countering the effects of destructive criticism: The relative efficacy of four interventions. *Journal of Applied Psychology, 75,* 235–245.

Beck, A. T., Brown, G., Berchick, R. J., Stewart, B. L., & Steer, R. A. (1990). Relationship between hopelessness and ultimate suicide. *American Journal of Psychiatry, 147,* 190–195.

Beck, A. T., & Freeman, A. (1990). *Cognitive therapy of personality disorders.* New York: Guilford Press.

Beck, A. T., & Young, J. E. (1985). Depression. In D. H. Barlow (Ed.), *Clinical handbook of psychological disorders* (pp. 206–244). New York: Guilford Press.

Behrens, D. (1990, September 21). Test-tube baby in tug-of-war. *New York Newsday,* pp. 3, 23.

Blakeslee, S. (1992a, January 7). Scientists unraveling chemistry of dreams. *The New York Times,* pp. C1, C10.

Blakeslee, S. (1992b, January 22). An epidemic of genital warts raises concern but not alarm. *The New York Times,* p. C12.

complex and troubling issue to most of us, and people on all sides of the issue share deep, sincere convictions." In this way, you recognize your audience's earnestness and get them involved. You can develop your particular viewpoints later.

If you are writing a journal article for professional colleagues, follow APA guidelines to the letter. Be concise, clear, and organized.

Write Clearly and Simply

Most good writing is reasonably easy to read. Intelligent writing does not have to be hard to follow, such as a Henry James novel or a Shakespearean play. Unless your assignment is to write a Victorian novel or an Elizabethan play, do not try to manufacture an intricate style or several layers of meaning.

The *Publication Manual* of the American Psychological Association (4th ed.; APA, 1994) advises you to present your ideas in a logical order, express them smoothly, and choose your words carefully. The table that follows provides examples of writing that lacks clarity and simplicity and of changes that make the examples clearer, simpler, and at least some better.

AWFUL	BETTER
Psychologists have engaged in complex correlational studies among peoples of diverse cultural subgroups to ascertain whether or not various variables related to the types of stimulation received in the home have effects on children's performance on intelligence tests and in the school.	Psychologists have correlated features of the home environment with the IQ scores and achievements of children from diverse ethnic groups.
Tyrants may arrive at the point where the recipients of their despotism are no longer swayed by their inhumanity.	People may lose their fear of tyrants.
In your writing, it is a good idea to keep your sentences as simple as you can reasonably do.	Keep sentences simple.
There are many different views and controversies surrounding the ethical nature of punishment and its effects on children's behavior in the school setting.	There is controversy concerning the ethics and efficacy of punishment in the school setting.

Be Willing to Make Mistakes

Failure is the condiment that gives success its flavor.

—TRUMAN CAPOTE

No college student is a perfect writer. Everyone makes mistakes. If you did not make mistakes, you would not need an education. The idea is to learn from your errors. When some aspect of a writing exercise is marked as poor, or wrong, make sure that you understand why so that you do not repeat the mistake.

Keep a Notebook or Journal

Creative writers, journalism students, and English majors are encouraged to keep notebooks to record important thoughts as they occur. You can practice this as well. For example, writers sometimes record the events around them—the heavy sky that threatens to burst into a storm or the suspended animation of a frozen January hillside—at other times, they record their innermost thoughts and feelings.

As a psychology student, you may want to keep a journal in which you note people's behavior under various circumstances. How do you and other people respond to stress? How do you feel when you think you are "in love"? How do you respond to a film or a television show? Jot down conditions that make it easier for you to learn academic material. Consider your motives for doing things and your responses to your successes and failures. You may also record potential psychological research studies that occur to you.

Logically Determine the Length of a Paper

Students are perpetually concerned about the length of a paper; that is, how long should a paper be? The correct answer is simple in principle, but it leaves many students dissatisfied. Generally speaking, the right number of words is the minimal number of words it takes to do the job. Again, the *Publication Manual* of the American Psychological Association (4th ed.; APA, 1994) urges frugality with words—"economy of expression." Put another way: Everything else being equal, a briefer paper or research report is better than a longer paper.

If you are not sure how long a paper should be, ask the professor or review previous papers that earned high grades. If the professor is not specific about numbers of words or pages, perhaps he or she can give you an impression of how long it should take to write the paper. Is it a paper that you should be able to write in one afternoon or one evening? Perhaps that would be two to five pages long (typed, double-spaced). Is it a term paper that requires a few days of library work and a few more days of writing? If so, 20 to 30 typewritten, double-spaced pages (including footnotes and bibliography) might be in order.

In any case, if the instructor specifies the number of pages for an assignment, be sure to comply. Failure to do so, even by a few pages, can result in a lower grade.

Avoid Plagiarism

> *I found your essay to be good and original. However, the part that was original was not good and the part that was good was not original.*
>
> —SAMUEL JOHNSON

Plagiarism derives from the Latin *plagiarius,* which roughly translates as "kidnapper" in English. Plagiarism is literary theft—the stealing of another person's ideas or words and passing them off as your own.

Let's be honest. Some students intentionally steal other people's work. They pass off a paper that was written by a fraternity brother 8 years ago as their own, or they copy passages of books verbatim. Students are not the only plagiarists. News reports now and then carry charges of plagiarism by film scriptwriters or politicians. Architecture students have even been known to steal designs from magazines.

Other students plagiarize inadvertently, however. The penalties for plagiarism can be severe. Failing the paper is a minimal penalty; plagiarizers can also fail the course. Occasionally, students are pressured to withdraw from college as a result of plagiarism. Stiff penalties seem appropriate for purposeful plagiarism. It is a pity to suffer them, however, for accidental plagiarism.

Professors may not be able to determine whether students have adapted or copied the papers of other students. It is relatively easy, however, for professors to discern whole passages that have been taken from books or articles. The passage may show a level of literary sophistication that exceeds that of the great majority of students. There may be a cogent recounting of facts that could be created only by an expert in the field. There may also be obvious inconsistencies in the paper: The student's own writing may struggle for clarity, whereas pilfered passages shine through.

The following guidelines will enable you to avoid the pitfalls and penalties of plagiarism:

1. When you mention other people's ideas or theories, attribute the ideas to their proper source. Write, for example,

   Abnormal behavior affects everyone in one way or another (Nevid, Rathus, & Greene, 2000). If we confine our definition of abnormal behavior to traditional psychological disorders—anxiety, depression, schizophrenia, abuse of alcohol and other drugs, and the like—perhaps one in three of us have been affected (Robins et al., 1984). If we include sexual dysfunctions and difficulties adjusting to the demands of adult life, many more are added. If we extend our definition to include maladaptive or self-defeating behavior patterns like compulsive gambling and dependence on nicotine, a clear majority of us are affected. (Nevid et al., 2000)

2. When you use other people's words, either place them in quotation marks or indent the material. Let length be your guide. When a passage runs from a few words to about four lines, use quotation marks. If a passage runs to five or more lines, indent the material similarly to the way I indented the preceding material on abnormal behavior. Whether you use quotation marks or indent, note the source of the material, including the page number or numbers on which it is found.

3. Generally, you can use a brief string of words (such as two or three) from your source without using quotation marks. Use quotation marks, however, if one of the words is a technical term or shows a fine literary turn of phrase—something you might not have arrived at on your own.

4. Keep the outline (if you used one) and the working drafts of your paper. If you are falsely accused of plagiarism, you can trace the development of your ideas and your phrasing.

Pick a Topic

You say there is nothing to write about. Then write to me that there is nothing to write about.

—PLINY THE YOUNGER

There are no dull subjects. There are only dull writers.

—H. L. MENCKEN

Professors may assign concrete topics, such as a reaction to a piece of writing, or provide a list of topics from which you must choose. Sometimes professors purposefully leave topics wide open. Professors may also assign a paper on some aspect of a topic, which tends to leave the decision pretty much to the student.

There are no hard-and-fast rules to picking a topic. Overall, however, writers—including college students—tend to be at their best on subjects with which they are familiar. The following list considers some motives for picking topics and ways to make them manageable:

- Write on Things You Know About

I should not talk so much about myself if there were anybody else whom I knew as well.

—HENRY DAVID THOREAU

The first novels of writers tend to be autobiographical in nature. This is true, in part, because writers seek ways of expressing their own ideas and making sense out of their own experiences. It is also true because it is helpful to write on things you know about. When you do this, you can devote more of your energies to the writing itself and relatively less to research. Also, we tend to think more deeply and critically about things with which we are familiar. All else being equal, essays about the familiar may impress the instructor as more sophisticated than essays about unfamiliar topics.

• Write About Things That Interest You

The best way to become acquainted with a subject is to write a book about it.

—BENJAMIN DISRAELI

Another motive for writing is to help you learn and organize your thoughts about an interesting topic. Return to the abortion issue. You may have strong ideas about abortion but little or no knowledge of the legal issues involved or the history of the pro-life and pro-choice movements. You could thus focus on historic and legal issues as a way of expanding your knowledge of the subject.

Perhaps you are intrigued by environmental psychology. Consider environmental issues such as acid rain or the greenhouse effect. You may have heard that the earth is undergoing a warming trend (greenhouse effect) because of certain emissions, but you may have little or no idea as to what emissions are. You could write a paper on the greenhouse effect as a way of becoming familiar with the atmospheric effects of various chemicals, the sources of these chemicals, and scientific and political efforts to control their emission.

Delimit the Topic

There is usually no magical fit between a topic and a theme paper of, say, 400 words or a term paper of 25 typewritten pages. However, you must make the topic fit. Although you may sometimes be at a loss for words, it may be easier to expand an apparently small topic to term paper size than to cut a broad topic down to size.

Are you interested in writing a paper on the "nature" of motivation? (If so, perhaps you should take out an insurance policy that protects you from sheer exhaustion.)

As a first step, you could choose between a paper on, for example, general theories of motivation, a paper that reviews theories of topics in motivation (e.g., a paper on theories of hunger, theories of thirst, or theories of homosexuality), or a paper that is limited to a more circumscribed area within a topic (e.g., the effects of the contemporary image of the ideal female figure on eating disorders). The last topic could be delimited further to only address anorexia nervosa.

If you find that there is too much literature to cover for a brief assignment, you may "trim" a topic on general theories of motivation to contemporary cognitive theories of aggression. In doing so, you delimit general theories to contemporary cognitive theory and motivation to one area of motivated behavior—aggression.

Write a Thesis Statement

If you are writing an argumentative theme paper, it is helpful to clarify your purpose through a thesis statement. A thesis is a proposition that is maintained or defended in an argument. Once you have narrowed your topic, try to express the thesis of your paper as briefly as possible—in a single sentence, if you can. You do not have to include the thesis statement in your paper. Instead, you can pin it up on the wall and use it as a guide in writing. A thesis statement helps to keep you from straying; it channels your arguments and evidence toward a goal.

If you are writing about abortion, for example, your thesis statement could be "Abortion is the taking of a human life," or "The individual woman has a right to exercise control over the events occurring inside her body." If you are writing about the effects of the contemporary image of the ideal female figure on eating disorders, your thesis statement could be "Contemporary images of women in the media are connected with a vast increase in the incidence of anorexia nervosa."

Do Not Wait for Inspiration—Get Going!

"Where shall I begin, please your Majesty?" he asked.
"Begin at the beginning," the King said, gravely, "and go on till you come to the end: then stop."

—LEWIS CARROLL, *ALICE IN WONDERLAND*

The idea is to get the pencil moving quickly.

—BERNARD MALAMUD

The idea of "getting going" is not elementary or silly, even if it sounds that way. Many students become bogged down soon after they select a topic (as do many professional writers!).

Getting going can mean going to the library and beginning to research the topic. Getting going can mean making an outline. Getting going can mean following inspiration and jotting down the introduction, some of the conclusions, or some of the ideas that you will probably use in the body of the paper. You can write down ideas on index cards or on loose-leaf pages that you can reorder later. If you are using a word processor, you can save random thoughts in separate files and integrate them later. You can also save them in the same file and then move them around as blocks of text when writing your paper.

The point is this: You have got to get going somewhere and at some time. If you have no plan at all, spend a few minutes to formulate a plan. If you have a plan and some useful thoughts come to you, feel free to stray from the plan and record these thoughts. It is easier to return to a plan than to reconstruct moments of inspiration!

For most of us, writing, similar to invention, is 10% inspiration and 90% perspiration. You cannot force inspiration. You can only set the stage for inspiration by delving into your topic—perhaps by formulating a plan (e.g., beginning with library work), writing an outline, or talking with other people about the topic. Then, when inspiration strikes, jot it down. Also keep this in mind: A good paper does not have to be inspired. A good paper can address the topic in a coherent, useful way without bursts of genius, without poetry. In fact, if you adhere to the recommendations in the *Publication Manual* of the American Psychological Association (4th ed.; APA, 1994), poetry is largely out of fashion.

Make an Outline

With nearly any kind of writing, it is helpful to make an outline. Short stories and novels profit from outlines of their plots and characters. Even brief essays of the sort you may write on a test profit from a listing of the issues to be raised or topics to be covered. With term papers, most students find it essential not only to list the topics that are to be covered, but also to sketch out how they will be covered.

Outlines usually take the following form:

I. Major head
  A. Second-level head
  B. Second-level head
    1. Third-level head
      a. Fourth-level head
      b. Fourth-level head
    2. Third-level head

Psychology articles have introductions and methods, results, and discussion sections. Theme papers and term papers have a beginning (introductions), a middle (bodies), and an end (conclusions). In writing theme papers and term papers, students can use a major head for the paper's introduction, one or more major heads for the body of the paper, and another major head for the conclusion.

You are now taking an introductory psychology course. In the future you may take a developmental psychology course, a human sexuality course, or a health course. In any of these classes, you might be writing a term paper on ways of coping with infertility. Your outline could look similar to that in Figure 2.

Compose a Draft

A draft is a rough or preliminary sketch of a piece of writing. One way to write a draft of an article, theme paper, or term paper is to flesh out an outline of the paper. Another way is to start writing the sections you know most about, or have the strongest feelings about, and then assemble them like you would a puzzle. Still another way is to just start writing, without even a mental outline, and somehow arrive at what seems to be a completed work.

Assume that you are using an outline and consider, in Figure 2, how you might flesh it out, section by section.

INTRODUCTION TO THE PAPER

If you can't annoy somebody, there's little point in writing.

—KINGSLEY AMIS

The introduction to a psychology article states the problem, briefly reviews previous research in the area, and shows how your research or theoretical discussion will test or answer some of the issues in the area.

The introduction to a theme paper or a term paper has similar functions. It presents issues you will discuss but may also aim to arouse the interest of the reader (and the instructor!). You may want to include your thesis statement within the introduction (i.e., "It will be shown that . . . "), but it is not necessary. If you are going to wax poetic in a paper, the beginning is a good place to start. Here are just a few of the ways in which writers grab the reader's interest:

1. Use an anecdote (e.g., as with the plight of Maggie).

2. Use an interesting piece of information from within the paper (e.g., "One American couple in six cannot conceive a child.").

3. Couple a fact with irony (e.g., "Despite the concern of environmentalists that we are witnessing a population explosion, one American couple in six cannot conceive a child." Or, "In an era when we are inundated with news about the high incidence of teenage pregnancy, one American couple in six cannot conceive a child.").

4. Use a quote from literature (e.g., "In Genesis 3:16 it is written, 'In sorrow thou shalt bring forth children.' Sad to say, it is the sorrow of one American couple in six that they shall *not* be able to bring forth children." This example combines a Biblical quote, irony, and a play on words—that is, the double use of the word *sorrow* and pointing out that so many parents will *not* bear ["bring forth"] children.).

5. Use a rhetorical question ("Did you know that one American couple in six cannot conceive a child?" Or, "Did you know that many couples who delay marriage and childbearing in an effort to establish careers are playing

FIGURE 2

Partial outline for term paper on "Ways of Coping with Infertility"

I. Introduction
   A. Attention getter (Maggie's story)
   B. Extent of the problem
   C. What I will do in this paper
II. Sources of infertility
   A. Problems that affect the male
      1. Low sperm count
      2. Irregularly shaped sperm
      3. Low sperm motility
      4. Infectious diseases
      5. Trauma or injury
      6. Autoimmune response
   B. Problems that affect the female
      1. Lack of ovulation
         a. Hormonal irregularities
         b. Malnutrition
         c. Stress
      2. Obstructions or malfunctions of the reproductive tract
      3. Endometriosis
         a. Special problems of "yuppies"
III. Methods for overcoming infertility
   A. Methods for overcoming male fertility problems
      1. Methods for overcoming low sperm count
         a. Artificial insemination
         b. Etc.
   B. Methods for overcoming female fertility problems
      1. Methods for overcoming lack of ovulation
      2. Methods for overcoming obstructions or malformations
         a. In vitro fertilization
         b. Gamete intra fallopian transfer (GIFT)
         c. Zygote intra fallopian transfer (ZIT)
         d. Donor IVF
         e. Etc.
      3. Methods for overcoming endometriosis
IV. Psychological issues
V. Financial issues
VI. Legal/moral issues
VII. Conclusions
   A. Brief review (summary)
   B. Conclusions (points to be made)
   C. Future questions or directions

Russian roulette with fertility?"). A so-called rhetorical question is not really meant to be answered. It is intended as an attention-grabbing way of leading into a topic.

You can also leave the writing of the important beginning lines of the paper until the end, when you have a greater grasp of the subject and are more acquainted with the issues involved. Of course, you are free to write down notes about possible beginnings as you work on other parts of the paper—whenever inspiration strikes.

Then the introduction can explain the issues that will be covered in the paper and how the paper will approach the topic.

BODY OF THE PAPER The body of the paper is the meat of the paper. If you are criticizing a work of literature, a film, or an art exhibit, this is where you list the strengths and weaknesses of the work and support your views. If you are writing an argumentative theme, this is where you state your premises and explain your logic. If you are reviewing research, this is where you explain who did what, when, and how. If your paper explains a number of processes (e.g., methods for overcoming infertility), this is where you get down to the nuts and bolts.

In the body of the paper, you paint the details. If you are writing the term paper on infertility, in section II (according to your outline), you describe endometriosis and explore theories as to how endometriosis impairs fertility. In section VI, you may point out that surrogate mothers are the actual biological mothers of the children who are born to them and that courts are in conflict as to whether biological mothers can sign away their rights to their children. You could expand your coverage by exploring religious opinions on surrogate motherhood and other issues and devoting space to its psychological and legal ramifications.

Sometimes it seems that subject matter must be organized in a certain way. At other times, organization may appear more flexible. In the paper on infertility, the body began with a section on sources of infertility. There was then a section on methods of overcoming infertility, followed by sections on psychological and related issues. The body of the paper could also have been organized according to kinds of problems. Section II could have been labeled "Problems That Affect the Male." Subsection 1 of section II could still have discussed low sperm count. Sections within subsection 1, however, could have discussed (a) sources of low sperm count, (b) methods of overcoming low sperm count, and (c) psychological and (d) other issues involved in handling the problem in the prescribed ways. Section III could then have discussed problems that affect the female.

CONCLUSION OF THE PAPER The conclusion or discussion section of a paper may contain more than conclusions. Similar to the introduction, the conclusion has many functions. The introduction of a paper tells readers where they are going, whereas the conclusion tells them where they have been.

In the paper on infertility, the last part of your introduction tells readers where they are going. In the sample outline, the first part of the conclusion tells readers where they have been. The first part of the discussion or concluding section is an excellent place for summarizing or briefly reviewing the information presented in the body of the paper. In summarizing the body, you are not simply adding words—that is, "padding" to meet a length requirement. Instead, you are reminding the reader of the major points as a way of leading up to your judgments, inferences, or opinions.

Then you may arrive at the conclusions themselves. Your conclusions put everything in perspective. They explain what it all means. One conclusion of the paper on infertility could be that science is continually finding innovative ways of overcoming fertility problems. Another conclusion could be that these innovations have created new ethical and religious dilemmas. You could also take a personal ethical or religious stance, assuming that you label it as your view and do not equate it with eternal truth or majority opinion. Still another conclusion could be that certain aspects of modern life (e.g., toxins, delay of childbearing) contribute to infertility.

Ideally, the conclusion section ends with a bang. The beginning of a paper may attempt to grab the reader's interest, as does the ending sometimes also aim to achieve an impact. You can refer to future directions—perhaps the possibility that someday it may be possible to create a child by processing nearly any cell from the father and any cell from the mother. You can go for shock value with the notion that the parents could conceivably be of the same gender or that there might be only one parent (as in cloning). You can return to Maggie's suffering and suggest that would-be parents will no longer have to undergo her travails.

You can also speculate on how reproductive technology may have a wide impact on social, religious, and political institutions. In a more matter-of-fact mode, you can suggest new avenues of research. You can also use humor, irony, or rhetorical questions—the same devices that draw readers into papers.

The first few lines of the paper make your first impression. The last few lines make your final impression. These are the places where you want to make the greatest impact. If there are sentences you are going to work, work, and rework, let them be the first and last few sentences of the paper.

REVISE THE PAPER

> *It's none of their business that you have to learn how to write. Let them think you were born that way.*

> —ERNEST HEMINGWAY

> *I can't write five words but that I change seven.*

> —DOROTHY PARKER

Wolfgang Amadeus Mozart is the great musician who bridged the Baroque and Romantic movements. His musical compositions are distinctive not only for their majesty, but also because they were composed practically without revision. It is as though his original conception of his music was complete and flawless. He is a rarity in the world of music.

It is also rare in the world of writing that our original ideas are complete and flawless. There are many false starts, many bad passages. Good writing usually requires revision, sometimes many revisions, even when the writer is experienced. Revision is a natural part of the writing process. Frequently, revision spells the difference between a paper that deserves an "F" and one that earns an "A".

However, papers should not be revised just for the sake of revision. Now and then we may produce a first draft that we cannot improve. When this occurs, an old saying applies: "If it ain't broke, don't fix it."

There are revisions, and then there are revisions. Rarely is every sentence or even every section of a paper revised. Sometimes we revise papers to fine-tune our prose, to improve our sentence structure, or to reconsider our choice of words. This type of revising is referred to as *editing*, which means scrutinizing the paper word by word and changing words or sentences that are wrong, weak, or inappropriate. Editing extends to replacing words, sentences, and paragraphs with improved versions.

Sometimes we revise to reshape our ideas so that they fit together more coherently. At other times, we revise to fill gaps. At still other times, we labor to perfect our beginnings and endings.

A CLOSER LOOK

OVERCOMING A WRITING BLOCK

Ah, that blank sheet of paper! The possibilities are endless, so why can't you get something down?

All writers, not just college students, find themselves staring at that empty page now and then, wondering how to overcome a "writing block."

Imagine that you have picked a topic and have been staring at the page for half an hour. Nothing is coming to mind. What can you do? There are no certain answers, but here are some suggestions that have helped other students.

1. Brainstorm. In brainstorming, you do not try to narrow in on a single way to solve a problem. Instead, you generate as many kinds of approaches as possible. Set a time limit for your brainstorming. Then sit back and allow any relevant ideas to pop into mind, even outlandish ideas. Or ask roommates and friends for their ideas—even silly ones. During the session, just record ideas; don't judge them. When the session is finished, consider each idea and test those that seem most likely to be of help.

2. Take a break. Have a snack, call a friend, take a shower, or get on the rowing machine. Then get back to work. You may find that your ideas have incubated while you were taking your break. When we stand back from the problem for a while, a solution may later appear to us.

3. Work on another assignment. Instead of continuing to frustrate yourself, complete another assignment. Then return to the paper refreshed.

4. Force yourself to write. Make yourself write on the subject for a specific amount of time—for example, for 20 minutes. Try to develop the arguments in the paper. Then critically examine what you have written.

5. Switch tools. If you've been processing words on a personal computer, try a typewriter for a while or use longhand.

6. Skip to another section. Work on another section of the paper. Type up the reference list, for instance. (It's amazing how reviewing sources helps to generate ideas!) Or work on your "dynamite" opening paragraph.

7. Let the paper go for a few days. This alternative may help when a short break is ineffective and you still have plenty of time to complete the paper.

8. Check with the instructor. He or she may have some excellent advice for resuming the paper. Some instructors do not mind offering detailed suggestions.

9. Copy and go! Copy the last sentence or paragraph you wrote and just go with it! Or sketch four or five different directions you can take.

10. Accept reality? Sometimes you can't go on because your ideas are truly at a dead end. If the block persists, consider tossing out what you have written and starting from scratch. Perhaps you should change topics. If you have already written 20 pages or checked 50 sources, however, you may find it worthwhile to explore switching topics with your instructor before tossing it into the circular file (i.e., the wastebasket).

How much revision is enough? That depends on you as a writer, on the piece that you are writing, and on the expectations of your instructors. As you move more deeply into your college career, you will gain a more accurate impression of how much revision your work usually requires to satisfy your professors—and yourself.

Here are some specific suggestions for revising your papers:

1. Create distance between you and your work. Sometimes you need a bit of distance between yourself and your work to recognize weaknesses and errors. One good way to create this distance is to let time pass between drafts—at least a day. In this way, you may be able to look at certain passages or ideas from a new perspective. Of course, you cannot use this method if you do not begin a term paper until a few days before it is due! Another method is to have a trusted friend, family member, or tutor at the college learning center review the paper. Then you must try to listen to suggestions with an unbiased ear.

2. Check the draft against the outline. Are there obvious omissions? Have you strayed from the topic?

3. Place earlier drafts beside you as you write. Start writing from scratch, but follow the earlier versions as you proceed. Use segments of earlier versions that seem right. Omit sections that are weak or incorrect.

4. Set aside earlier drafts and sketch a new version. After you sketch a new version, compare it with earlier drafts and incorporate the strengths of each version.

5. Read the draft aloud. When we listen to ourselves, we sometimes gain a new perspective on what we are saying—or not saying. This is another way to create a bit of distance between our writing and us. You can also try reading the paper aloud to a friend.

6. Try a new direction. If something is not working, consider taking a different approach. It is not unusual, for example, to change a thesis statement after completing a draft of a paper. You may also find that you need to explore a different kind of research.

7. Drop passages that do not work. Dropping passages may be the hardest piece of advice to follow. It is painful to throw a piece of work into the wastebasket, especially if we have devoted hours to it. Yet, not every effort is of high quality. *One of the important differences between artists and hacks is that artists are more willing to acknowledge their failures and toss them onto the scrap heap.*

8. Ask the instructor for advice. Drop by during office hours and share some of your concerns with the instructor. You will not only help to organize your own thoughts but will also show respect for the instructor's time when you preplan your questions and make them fairly concrete. Do not say, "I think something's wrong with my paper, but I don't know what." Say, instead, "My thesis was A, but the research seems to be showing B. Should I modify the thesis? Have I hit the right research?" By asking the instructor for advice, you do not appear weak and dependent. Instead, you appear sincere and interested in self-improvement. This is precisely the attitude that your instructor respects.

USING A WORD PROCESSOR Professor Jacqueline Berke at Drew University notes that because of word processing,

> [Our] understanding of the way people write—the stages—the process—has changed. The phase of writing that is actually most important is revision. Yet how much time does the poor student give to revision? She remembers a comment from a student's journal: "The computer makes revision a playground instead of a punishment." (Boyer, 1987, pp. 171–172).

A good word processing program can help you in many ways. For example,

1. The single greatest advantage to word processing is that you can edit a manuscript indefinitely without having erasures, arrows, and scrawls between the lines. With every change, the material on the screen is brand new. The actual mechanics of making changes are relatively effortless and do not compromise your desire to achieve perfection.

2. You can save each draft of a paper for future reference. For example, in the paper on infertility, the outline could be saved as "INFERT.OUT" or as "Infertility Outline March 10, 2001." The first draft could be saved as "INFERT.D1" or as "Infertility Draft 1 March 18, 2001." Subsequent drafts can be numbered and dated. Students should always make and keep copies of the papers that they submit. When you use word processing, you save your papers electronically on hard drives or floppy disks. Each copy of the paper is an original (called a "hard copy" or "display copy"), and you can generate as many original copies as you want.

3. In case the question arises as to whether your paper is original—that is, written by you—copies of each draft can be produced as evidence.

4. You can save related thoughts or abstracts of research studies in separate files and integrate them later.

5. Many word processing programs automatically renumber all footnotes or endnotes when you insert a new entry.

6. Many word processing programs check the spelling for you. Such programs catch the following errors:

    I shall show that Woody Allen's recent <u>tradegies</u> are less <u>successfull</u> than his early comedies as works of art.

    Note though that spell-checking programs do not catch errors such as the following:

    I shall show <u>than</u> Woody Allen's recent tragedies <u>art</u> less <u>successfully that</u> his early comedies as <u>words on</u> art.

    However, grammar-checking programs may catch such errors.

7. Many word processing programs have a thesaurus that allows you to conveniently search for better wording.

Proofread the Paper

A man occupied with public or other important business cannot, and need not, attend to spelling.

—NAPOLEON BONAPARTE

I know not, madam, that you have a right, upon moral principles, to make your readers suffer so much.

—SAMUEL JOHNSON, LETTER TO MRS. SHERIDAN,
AFTER PUBLICATION OF HER NOVEL IN 1763

This is the sort of English up with which I will not put.

—SIR WINSTON CHURCHILL

Napoleon was probably powerful enough, of course, that few people would have brought misspellings to his attention. Most of us do not have the prerogatives of Napoleon. Proofreading is intended to catch the kinds of errors that make many professors groan and, in Johnson's words, "suffer so much." Proofreading is a form of editing directed at catching errors in spelling, usage, and punctuation, instead of enhancing the substance of the paper. Proofreading is generally not a creative process; it is more mechanical. However, if in proofreading you discover that a word does not accurately express your intended meaning, a bit of creativity might be needed to replace it or recast the sentence.

IMPORTANCE OF PROOFREADING

I will not go down to posterity talking bad grammar.

—BENJAMIN DISRAELI (CORRECTING ONE
OF HIS MANUSCRIPTS ON HIS DEATHBED)

For a largely mechanical process, proofreading is extremely important. For example, poor spelling and sentence structure suggest ignorance. Whether the instructor states that attention will be paid to spelling and so forth, you may still be judged by the mechanics. That is, an instructor who believes that you cannot spell may also believe that you cannot write a good paper.

When a paper has mechanical errors, the message to the instructor is very clear: You do not care enough to proofread the paper yourself or to have it proofread by someone who knows the mechanics.

Many campuses have tutorial centers at which you can have your papers proofread without charge. You may have various reasons for not using the tutorial service: unwillingness to have your work scrutinized by others (even though your instructor will be doing so), lack of time or inconvenient location (which is more inconvenient in the long run—writing the paper in time to have it proofread or receiving a poorer grade than necessary?), or simply not caring. Whatever your reason for failing to proofread your paper, your instructor will interpret the flaws as signs of (a) lack of knowledge and (b) not caring—leading to lack of effort. Lack of knowledge and lack of effort are the two major reasons for poor grades on papers.

However, do not expect a proofreader to catch every error. Most tutors, for example, point out errors but do not make corrections themselves. Moreover, having a tutor check your paper does *not* remove your responsibility for catching and correcting errors, nor does it guarantee that all errors have been highlighted. So do not blame your tutor for your own errors. The best way to work with a tutor is to have him or her read over your paper and offer suggestions at various stages of the paper's development. You should also be striving to learn rules for proper usage—not just to catch the errors in a single paper.

TIPS FOR PROOFREADING The following guidelines will help you to proofread successfully:

1. When proofreading, read your paper letter by letter, word by word, phrase by phrase, and punctuation mark by punctuation mark. (Some English professors recommend starting at the end of your paper and reading it backward, sentence by sentence, as a way of catching small errors.) Do not focus on issues such as poetic value and persuasiveness of arguments. Pay attention to the littlest things. Are you using slang words to add color and help make your arguments, or are you just careless?

2. Check whether your tenses are consistent. Are you saying "Tolman *noted* (past tense) that . . ." in one place and "Tolman *argues* (present tense) that . . ." in another?

3. Check for subject-verb agreement. *Everyone* is a singular pronoun. Did you write "Everyone in *their* (plural) right mind . . ." when you should have written "Everyone in her or his right mind . . ."?

4. Check that sentences are, in fact, sentences, and not fragments or run-ons. If you are using sentence fragments occasionally, be certain that they help to

highlight your points (e.g., "Not likely!") and do not reflect carelessness. Use fragments purposefully, not by accident.

5. Have a trusted friend proofread your papers in exchange for you proofreading your friend's papers. A page may look correct to you because you are used to looking at it; however, errors might leap off the page upon perusal by someone else.

6. When in doubt, use the dictionary.

7. Check that your footnotes and references or bibliography contain the information required by your professor and are in the specified format. For most students taking introductory psychology courses, the correct format will be APA format.

8. Be certain that you have credited your sources so that you are not suspected or accused of plagiarism.

9. At the risk of being boring, I repeat: If the learning center at your college offers a proofreading service, use it.

PROOFREAD TO CORRECT BIASED LANGUAGE The profession of psychology champions the dignity of the individual human, whether that person is a man or a woman, younger or older, or with or without a psychological disorder.

For example, sexist language is usually biased in favor of men. When talking about a person whose gender is ambiguous, for example, sexist language uses the pronouns *he, him,* and *his.* When referring to people or to humans in general, sexist language uses the noun *man* or *mankind.*

Sexist language also stereotypes people, as in the usage *woman physician* rather than merely *physician.* (The point in the last example is that the writer is suggesting that physicians tend to be men; therefore, the gender must be specified when the physician is a woman.)

The American Psychological Association (1994) also points out many other examples of bias in language. For example, the traditional use of terms such as *subjects, receiving treatments, schizophrenics,* and *the elderly* denies individuals their dignity and their active participation in research. The APA therefore recommends that we speak of *individuals, people,* and *participants*—not of *subjects.* We should speak of individuals as active in research—as *partaking* in research or as *obtaining* treatments, not as *receiving* treatments. We should use "people first" language, speaking of *people with schizophrenia* or *people diagnosed with schizophrenia,* not of *schizophrenics.* We should write *older people,* not *the elderly.* In all our writings, the person should always come first. It is the person that defines the individual. The modifier, whether it refers to age, psychological disorders, or other matters, is secondary. This is not verbal game playing. People are people and deserve to be treated with dignity regardless of age, psychological disorder, or participation in research. Our descriptors expand or limit the nature of other humans, and psychology teaches us that people deserve our consideration.

Table 2 offers examples of biased language and suggestions for correcting it. It is based on the guidelines for reducing biased language as suggested by the American Psychological Association (1994).

PROOFREAD TO CORRECT COMMON ERRORS IN USAGE
Proofread to correct common errors in usage as well. Consider this piece of romantic dialog:

"I love you alot," said Marsha, "accept when you're mean to me."

"Just among you and I," John responded, "I'm alright when I'm laying down. You should of known that standing up gives me a headache. Anyways, I didn't no that I had that affect on you."

TABLE 2

EXAMPLES OF BIASED LANGUAGE AND HOW TO CORRECT THEM

BIASED USAGE	SUGGESTED ALTERNATIVES
A research subject is required to give *his* informed consent.	A participant in research is required to give informed consent. (*Subject* is changed to *participant* and *his* is deleted.)
	A participant in research is required to give *his* or *her* informed consent. (*or her* is added.)
	A participant in research is required to give *her* or *his* informed consent. (Better yet! Varies the traditional practice of putting the man first.)
	Participants in research are required to give *their* informed consent. (Plural form is used.)
	Informed consent is requested from research participants. (Sentence is recast.)
Psychology has advanced our knowledge of *man* (or *mankind*).	Psychology has advanced our knowledge of *humans* (or *human beings*, or *humanity*, or *people*, or *the human species*).
Policeman, fireman, mothering, chairman, freshman or freshmen, girls, Mrs. John Doe	Police *officer*, fire *fighter*, *parenting*, *chair* or chair*person*, *first-year student(s)*, *women* (unless very young), *Jane Doe*
The study focused on *schizophrenics*.	The study focused on *people diagnosed with schizophrenia*. (People participate in the study, and they should not be stereotyped according to a psychological disorder.)
Control subjects did not *receive* a treatment.	*Individuals in the control group* did not *obtain* the treatment. (The term *subjects* denies people their dignity; it is preferable to speak of *people* or *individuals in a control group*. We can also be more specific; for example, we can say *children in the control group* or *people diagnosed with panic disorder in the control group*. To say that people *receive* a treatment is to portray them as victims and, again, to deny their dignity. It is therefore preferable to say that people *obtain* a treatment or *participate in* a treatment. We can be more specific here as well; for example, we can say that individuals in the control group *drank* water only, rather than that they *received* water only.)
Blacks are more likely than *whites* to *suffer* from hypertension.	*African Americans* are more likely than *White Americans* to be diagnosed with hypertension. (The American Psychological Association [1994] suggests using the terms *African American* and *White American*. Such terms are not hyphenated. In some instances, it may be advisable to use the word *Black*, however [as in *Black South Africans* and *White South Africans*].
Oriental people	Use *Asians* (for people in Asia) or *Asian Americans*. Or be more specific and use *Japanese Americans* or *Chinese Americans*.
The study focused on the problems of *the elderly*.	The study focused on the problems of *older people*.
Homosexuality	Use *a gay male* or *lesbian sexual orientation*. [The term *homosexuality* is unclear in meaning (i.e., does it refer to a sexual orientation or to behavior) and has become connected with stereotyping and prejudice.]
Homosexual behavior	Use *male–male sexual behavior* or *female–female sexual behavior*. (Confuses sexual orientation with behavior.)
Homosexuals	Use *gay males and/or lesbians*.

All right, I confess, no student of mine ever wrote anything this awful. I had to piece together multiple errors to arrive at this gem.

Table 3 alerts you to a number of common usage errors. Look for them as you proofread your paper. The table could have been endless; however, I chose to focus on some errors that are likely to make instructors think that students might be better off working in a car wash than taking a course in psychology.

TABLE 3

COMMON ERRORS IN ENGLISH USAGE AND HOW TO CORRECT THEM	
SOURCE OF CONFUSION	**CLARIFICATION**
Confusing *accept* and *except*	*Accept* is a verb meaning "to receive favorably" or "to approve," as in "accepting someone's point of view" or "accepting someone's application to a graduate program in psychology(!)." *Except* can be a verb, meaning "to leave out" or a preposition meaning "leaving out," as in "They invited everyone except me."
Confusing *advice* and *advise*	*Advice* is a noun, something that is given, as in "This is my advice to you." *Advise* is a verb, meaning "to counsel" or "to give advice," as in "I would advise you to be cautious."
Confusing *affect* and *effect*	Most of the time, *affect* is a verb meaning "to stir or move the emotions" or "to influence." Consider this example: "I was affected by the movie." Most of the time, *effect* is a noun meaning "something brought about by a cause," as in the phrase "cause and effect." Consider this example: "The movie had an enormous effect on me." *Affect* is also used as a noun, but usually only by psychologists and other people who work with individuals who have psychological disorders. In that case, it is pronounced AF-fect and means "an emotion or emotional response." *Effect* is also occasionally used as a verb, meaning "to bring about or produce a result," as in "to effect change."
Confusing *affective* and *effective*	*Affective* means "of feelings" or "of emotions." Disorders currently referred to as *mood disorders* in the Diagnostic and Statistical Manual (DSM) of the American Psychiatric Association were previously termed *affective disorders.* Unless you are talking about such disorders, you are more likely to be thinking of the word *effective,* meaning "having an effect" or "producing results." Consider this example: "Lisa made an effective speech."
Confusing *all right* and *alright*	Use *all right. Alright* is technically incorrect, and the Third College Edition of *Webster's New World Dictionary* (Simon & Schuster, 1988) lists "alright" as a variant spelling of "all right," whose usage is disputed. If your instructor marks "all right" wrong (which sometimes happens!), see him or her during office hours, pull out your dictionary, and be a hero. Be nice, not snide! All right?
Confusing *allot, alot,* and *a lot*	Use *a lot* if you mean "many, plenty" or "a great deal." *Allot* (with two *l*'s) is a verb meaning "to apportion" or "to distribute." There is no such word as *alot.* Some instructors may take issue with your ever using *a lot* as well. They may say that "A lot is a piece of land" and ask that you use "much" or "many" instead.
Confusing *all ready* and *already*	*All ready* means "everyone" or "everything" is "ready," as in "We are all ready to get into the car" or "Dinner is all ready." *Already* means "done previously," as in "I wrote the paper already" or "The paper is already finished."
Confusing *allude, elude,* and *illude*	*Allude* means "to refer," as in "I alluded to Skinner's *Walden II* in my paper." *Elude* means "to avoid" or "to escape," as in "He eluded the enemy." There is no such word as illude.
Confusing *allusion* and *illusion*	An *allusion* is a reference, as in "I made an allusion to Rogers' *Client-Centered Therapy.*" An *illusion* is "a false idea or conception" or "a misleading appearance." Consider this example: "The Ponzo illusion apparently depends on our tendency to assume that the sloping lines are parallel and receding into the distance."
Confusing *all together* and *altogether*	*All together* means "all in the same place" or "all at once," as in "Let's try singing that song again, all together this time." *Altogether* means "completely," as in "I'm altogether disgusted with the way you did that."
Confusing *among* and *between*	*Among* is used when there are three or more people or objects. *Between* is usually used when there are two people or objects. "We had $10 between us" and "between you and me" is correct when two people are involved. "They distributed the money among us" is correct when three or more people have received the money.
Confusing *anymore* with *any more* and *anyplace* with *any place*	Each is always two words. (End of issue.)
Confusing *as* and *like*	As a preposition, *like* means "similar to" or "resembling," as in "The clouds look like cotton candy," or "This problem wasn't like the other problems." *As* usually means "to the same degree" ("The missile flew straight as a bullet") or "at the same time" ("He read as he watched television").

(continues)

TABLE 3

COMMON ERRORS IN ENGLISH USAGE AND HOW TO CORRECT THEM *(continued)*

SOURCE OF CONFUSION	CLARIFICATION
Confusing *backward* and *backwards*	Use either one! They mean the same thing and are both acceptable. (Enjoy the correctness of both options while you can; you don't have this freedom very often.)
Confusing *bad* and *badly*	*Bad* is an adjective that describes states of health and emotions, as in "He looked bad" and "She felt bad." The adverb *badly* describes actions, as in "He pitched the ball badly."
Confusing *can* and *may*	*Can* refers to ability, as in "Anything you can do I can do better." *May* refers to permission, as in "You may not break the law," and to probability, as in "That may or may not happen."
Confusing *cite, sight,* and *site*	*Cite* is a verb usually meaning "to quote" or "to refer to," as in "She cited the views of many researchers and theorists in her argument." *Sight* is eyesight or vision. A *site* is a piece of land, as in the "site of a work of architecture," or the place where something happens, as in "the site of a battle."
Confusing *complement* and *compliment*	To *compliment* means to praise, whereas to *complement* is to balance or complete.
Confusing *continual* and *continuous*	*Continuous* means without interruption, as in "The Earth's rotation is continuous." *Continual* means often, but with interruption, as in "His continual complaining depressed his spouse."
Confusing *credible* and *credulous*	*Credible* means believable, whereas a *credulous* person is gullible, or readily fooled.
Confusing *criteria* and *criterion*	*Criteria* is the plural of *criterion.* You will look very erudite when you use these words correctly in your written work!
Confusing *data* and *datum*	*Data* is a plural noun, and *datum* is singular. A *datum* is a single piece of information, whereas the "data obtained in a study" usually refers to the entire mass of information assembled. Because *data* is a plural noun, write "the data have implications," not "the data has implications."
Confusing *desert* and *dessert*	The *dessert* is the final course in a meal. *Desert* refers to arid land and, as a verb, means to abandon (e.g., "He deserted her in the desert, without dessert." (Hint: Remember that *s* stands for "sweet" and "dessert" has two *s*s because it's sweeter. [Ugh.])
Confusing *disinterested* and *uninterested*	*Disinterested* means impartial or unbiased; a judge should be *disinterested.* *Uninterested* means without interest; a judge should not be *uninterested.*
Confusing *emigrate* and *immigrate*	To *emigrate* is to leave a country; to *immigrate* is to enter a country.
Confusing *eminent* and *imminent*	*Eminent* means respected and well known, as in "The eminent psychologist engaged in original research." *Imminent* means soon to arrive, as in "imminent disaster."
Confusing *etc.* and *et al.*	*Etc.* is the abbreviation of *et cetera* and means "and so forth." For example, "The company ran over budget on salaries, paper clips, coffee cups, etc." *Et al.* is the abbreviation of *et alia,* meaning "and others." For most psychology students, use of *et al.* is limited to lists of authors, as in "In the study by Saeed et al., it was found that . . ." Note that the *al.* is followed by a period, whereas *et* is not.
Confusing *farther* and *further*	Today these words appear to be interchangeable, each one meaning "more distant or remote" or "additionally." *Farther* used to be limited in meaning to "more distant," however, as in "They ran farther," and *further* used to be limited to "additionally," as in "They further investigated the issue." You will probably look more sophisticated if you stick to the older usage. You can pull out your dictionary if your instructor takes issue with your usage.
Confusing *few* and *less*	*Few* and *fewer* are used with countable items, as in "We need fewer people in the room." *Less* refers to volume or extent, as in "I need less noise and aggravation."
Confusing *flammable* and *inflammable*	Despite the fact that the prefix *in-* usually means "not," both words have the same meaning: "capable of catching on fire."
Confusing *good* and *well*	*Good* is an adjective; *well* is the adverbial form of good. You look *good* [aren't we complimentary?] and you do things *well.* As an adjective, however, *well* means healthy. So "You look good" means you're attractive, but "You look well" means you seem healthy.

TABLE 3

COMMON ERRORS IN ENGLISH USAGE AND HOW TO CORRECT THEM *(continued)*

SOURCE OF CONFUSION	CLARIFICATION
Confusing *hanged* and *hung*	People are *hanged* (despite one's views on capital punishment) and coats are *hung*.
Confusing *have* and *of*	The confusion here usually occurs in contractions, such as *should've* or *could've*. When you can also use the verb *have*, use *'ve*, not the preposition *of*. Never write *could of*, *should of*, or *would of*. (Yes, I know I just wrote them, but I'm the author; I can get away with anything.)
Confusing *I* and *me*	*I* is the subject of a verb, as in "I am going" or "She and I are going." *Me* is the object of a preposition, as in "Give it to her and (to) me," or the object of a verb, as in "Don't discourage John and me."
Confusing *imply* and *infer*	To *imply* is to suggest, and to *infer* is to deduce or interpret. A literary passage may have *implications*, but readers draw their own *inferences*. Psychologists "draw inferences" from their data, but the data have implications.
Confusing *important* and *statistically significant*	The words *important* and *significant* are often synonymous. However, a *statistically significant* difference is a technical term that means "unlikely to be due to chance variation."
Confusing *irregardless* and *regardless*	The terms mean exactly the same thing, thus use the shorter (more parsimonious?) word, *regardless*. *Irregardless* is considered to be nonstandard usage and is technically incorrect.
Confusing *lie* and *lay*	This is where you make your mark! Many well-educated people cringe when they get stuck in a sentence that requires them to choose between the words. The verb *lie* means "recline," as in "Lie down" or "We have to lie low for a while." (*Lie* also means "to tell a lie," of course.) The verb *lay* means "put or place down" and always takes a direct object, as in "Lay the book (direct object) on the table." We also speak of "laying odds" (placing odds) for a bet, and *lay* is also considered a vulgar term for engaging in sexual activity.

The tenses of *lie* are as follows:

Present tense:	*Lie,* as in "I need to lie down," or "We intend to lie in wait right here."
Past tense:	*Lay,* as in "Earlier this morning I lay down for a while," or "This is where they lay in wait the other day."
Past participle:	*Lain,* as in "By the time dinner was ready, he had already lain down for a nap," or "They had lain in wait for six hours when the sun set."

The tenses of *lay* are as follows:

Present tense:	*Lay,* as in "Lay down your weapons [objects]," or "Please lay the foundation [object] for the building."
Past tense:	*Laid,* as in "They laid down their weapons," or "He laid the foundation for the building."
Past participle:	*Laid,* as in "They had already laid down their weapons" or "By the time the carpenters were ready, the foundation for the building had been laid."

Never, never (never) write or say "Lay down." Always use "Lie down."

SOURCE OF CONFUSION	CLARIFICATION
Confusing *leave* and *let*	*Leave* can mean "to go away"; "to cause to stay," as in "Leave some food"; and "to bequeath," as in "leaving money to one's children or charity." *Let* usually means "to allow," as in "Let me go" or "Let it be." (To *let* an apartment, however, is to rent it.)
Confusing *lend* and *loan*	*Lend* is a verb and *lent* is the past tense, as in "She lent me some money yesterday." *Loan* is preferably used as a noun, as in "She gave me a small loan." There is no such word as loaned.
Confusing *loose* and *lose*	*Loose* is an adjective, meaning the opposite of tight, as in "The knot came loose." *Lose* (pronounced looz) is the verb meaning "to misplace."
Confusing *mad* and *angry*	*Mad* means "insane" in formal usage, not angry. Persons with severe diagnosable psychological disorders might be mad in the sense of having uncontrollable impulses or being delusional. Still, they might be angry if dinner were served late.

(continues)

TABLE 3

COMMON ERRORS IN ENGLISH USAGE AND HOW TO CORRECT THEM *(continued)*	
SOURCE OF CONFUSION	**CLARIFICATION**
Confusing *media* and *medium*	The noun *medium* is singular; *media* is plural. Television is a medium. Television, cinema, and photography are media. The question, "What are the effects of media violence?", means "What are the effects of violence as shown on television, in films, etc.?" "Medium violence," if you would ever say such a thing, would refer to a moderate amount of violence.
Confusing *ones* and *one's*	*Ones* is a plural noun, as in "This column contains four ones." *One's* is possessive, as in "It is good to do one's own work" (I'm such a moralist). *One's* is also the contraction of one is.
Confusing *phenomena* and *phenomenon*	*Phenomena* is the plural form of *phenomenon*. (Memorize this one along with *criteria* and *criterion*.)
Confusing *principal* and *principle*	A *principal* is an important or central thing or person, as in "the principal museums of the United States" or the "principal of the primary school." A *principle* is a guiding rule, such as the Golden Rule ("Do unto others . . .").
Confusing *set* and *sit*	To *set* is "to arrange or put in place." *Set* takes a direct object, as in "Set the table [object]" or "Set the carton [object] down on the floor." To *sit* is "to be seated" or "to remain in place."
Confusing *shall* and *will*	These auxiliary verbs are used to show future tense ("They will be ready tomorrow") or to express determination or obligation ("You shall do what I tell you to do!"). The formal approach of showing the future tense is as follows: I *shall* go tomorrow You (singular) *will* go tomorrow He/she/it *will* go tomorrow We *shall* go tomorrow You (plural) *will* go tomorrow They *will* go tomorrow The formal approach to showing determination or obligation is as follows: I *will* get this done! You (singular) *shall* get this done! He/she/it *shall* get this done! We *will* get this done! You (plural) *shall* get this done! They *shall* get this done! Your instructor may have other ideas. Some instructors—even English instructors—feel that the formal approach to using these verbs is stuffy or out of touch with modern times. Do not be surprised if you write what is technically correct and are questioned about it. (Bring this book to your instructor during office hours so that I get blamed for it and not you.)
Confusing *stationary* and *stationery*	*Stationary* means "still" or "in one place," as in "In the autokinetic effect, a *stationary* object seems to move." *Stationery* is the paper on which you write.
Confusing *taught* and *taut*	*Taught* is the past tense of teach. *Taut* means "tight," as in "The rope is taut" or, metaphorically, "His nerves were strung taut."
Confusing *that* and *which*	Clauses that use the relative pronoun *that* are essential to the meaning of a sentence, as in "The subjects that learned the maze reached the food goal." Clauses that begin with the relative pronoun *which* add further information but are not essential to the meaning of the sentence, as in "The subjects, which had an opportunity to explore the maze, were not rewarded for their efforts."
Confusing *their*, *there*, and *they're*	*Their* is possessive, as in "They met their obligations." *There* shows location, as in "here and there." *They're* is the contraction of "they are."
Confusing *to*, *too*, and *two*	*To* is the preposition that shows location or destination, as in "Give the book to her" or "Go to school." *Too* is the adverb meaning "also," as in "I want to go, too," or "extremely," as in "That's too much!" *Two* is the number (2).

TABLE 3

COMMON ERRORS IN ENGLISH USAGE AND HOW TO CORRECT THEM *(continued)*	
SOURCE OF CONFUSION	**CLARIFICATION**
Confusing *toward* and *towards*	These prepositions have the same meaning and are both considered to be correct. I recommend using *toward* unless you are quoting someone's speech, in which case you would record what the person said or what you think the person would have said. (*Toward* is consistent with the *Publication Manual of the American Psychological Association's* (1994) suggestion that you use economy of expression.)
Confusing *use* and *utilize*	There is a slight difference in meaning between these words; to *utilize* is "to put to practical or profitable use." *Utilize* can make it seem that you are trying too hard, and you cannot make a mistake if you stick to *use*. In short, use *use* (economy of expression). Do not utilize *utilize*.
Confusing *while* and *although*	*While* connects events that are occurring simultaneously, as in "Food pellets dropped into the cage while the rat was pressing the lever." *Although* is used to mean "whereas" or "but," as in "Although Boyatsis (1974) found that students who drank alcohol behaved more aggressively, Lang (1975) found that students who believed they had drunk alcohol acted more aggressively, whether or not they had actually drunk alcohol."
Confusing *who* and *whom*	*Who* (or *whoever*) serves as the subject of a verb, as in "Who did this?!" *Whom* (or *whomever*) serves as the object of a preposition, as in "To (preposition) whom did you lend my car?" or as the object of a verb, as in "Choose (verb) whomever you prefer."
Confusing *whose* and *who's*	*Whose* is possessive, as in "Whose paper is this? It has no name!" *Who's* is the contraction of "who has" or "who is," as in the bear's lament, "Who's been sleeping in my bed?"
Confusing *your* and *you're*	*Your* is possessive, as in "This is your book." *You're* is the contraction of "you are," as in "I assume that you're going."

Produce the Final Copy

If you were applying for a job as a management trainee at a bank, would you arrive at the interview in unwashed jeans and a T-shirt? This is a rhetorical question as social psychology indicates that first impressions do count. First impressions also count with papers. I assume that you want to make a good first impression, to look like a serious contender, to put your best foot forward. You want your paper to look like a serious contender for an "A."

Here are some guidelines for producing and packaging the final copy:

1. Consider buying a plastic or paper binder for your paper. Use a binder that is serious and professional looking, not frivolous. For example, stiff brown paper and clear plastic are superior to lavender-tinted plastic.

2. Follow the specified format exactly. For most students taking this course, the format will be APA format. Sticking to the format does not guarantee a good grade but deviating from it will almost certainly hurt your grade.

3. If your professor does not specify a format, ask about his or her preferences.

4. Include a title or cover page (unless instructed not to do so). If your paper is a journal article or is required to look like one, follow the instructions for the title page given on page 8. If, however, you are designing your own title page, I advise including the following information:

Title of the paper

Your name

Title of the course

Name of your professor

Date of submission

5. *Spell the professor's name correctly.* You can find the proper spelling in the syllabus, college catalog, or—usually—on the door of the professor's office.

6. Learn the professor's preferred title (e.g., Ms., Dr.) and use it on the title page. A professor who has labored for many years to earn a doctorate may be justifiably annoyed if you do not write "Dr." on the title page.

7. If the paper is a term paper, include a table of contents.

8. Use good-quality white paper. Do not use lined paper, onion skin paper, or the cheapest quality copier paper.

9. Type your paper, double-spaced. (No excuses!)

10. Use black ink. Back in the days of the Model-T, it used to be said, "Make my car any color as long as it's black." (Instructors do not want to be distracted by the color of the ink. A color other than black suggests that you are not a serious student.)

11. Make sure the ribbon is new or nearly new, or that the toner is still black.

12. Use a standard typeface, such as pica or elite, courier or Times Roman (point size = 12). Use 10 or 12 characters to the inch. If you are going to be creative, do so in your formation of ideas and in your masterly usage of the English language—not in your typeface. If you are using word processing and a printer, choose a letter-quality (or near letter-quality) printer, not a dot matrix printer. (Do not cry poverty here until you have done some investigating and learned that your college cannot provide you with access to the printer that you need.)

13. Use margins of approximately 1 inch all around. Wider margins make a paper look skimpy. Narrower margins make a paper look cramped and hard to read. If you are using computer paper, carefully tear off the edges that contain the guiding holes.

14. Keep a copy of the paper. Professors may decide to hold on to some papers, and occasionally a paper does get lost.

HOW TO USE THE EXERCISES IN THIS BOOK

On the following pages are a number of issues and questions addressed in or related to the topics in your psychology textbook. Use principles of critical thinking to analyze each of them. Indicate whether you agree with the statements and answer the questions. If you disagree with a statement as it is written, perhaps you can draft a more carefully thought-out, accurate version.

In most cases, I try to get you started by offering some thoughts on how you might critically analyze the issue involved, but feel free to chart your own course if you prefer. Regardless of whose direction you follow—mine or your own—be skeptical, examine definitions of terms, weigh premises, examine the evidence, and consider whether the arguments are logical.

REFERENCES

American Psychological Association. (1994). *Publication manual of the American Psychological Association* (4th ed.). Washington, DC: Author.

Boyer, E. L. (1987). *College: The undergraduate experience in America.* New York: Harper & Row.

Kimble, G. A. (1994). A frame of reference for psychology. *American Psychologist, 49,* 510–519.

McGovern, T. (1989). Task force eyes the making of a major. *APA Monitor, 20*(7), 50.

Murray, B. (1997). Teaching today's pupils to think more critically. *APA Monitor, 28*(3), 51.

Nevid, J. S., Rathus, S. A., & Greene, B. (2000). *Abnormal psychology in a changing world* (4th ed). Upper Saddle River, NJ: Prentice Hall.

THINKING AND WRITING EXERCISES

PSYCHOLOGY AS A SCIENCE: UNDERSTANDING PEOPLE

EXERCISE 1: Do you believe that it is possible to understand people from a scientific perspective? Why or why not?

Can the richness and complexity of human behavior be reduced to scientific statements? What is human behavior? What is science?

Which, if any, aspects of human behavior seem subject to scientific analysis? Which, if any, do not?

_____

_____

_____

_____

_____

_____

_____

_____

_____

_____

PSYCHOLOGY AS A SCIENCE: WHO ARE THE PSYCHOLOGISTS?

EXERCISE 2: What characteristics or interests are shared by all psychologists? What kinds of characteristics or interests set different kinds of psychologists apart?

There are many different kinds of psychologists. Perhaps one way to address this question is by discussing psychologists' commonalities as scientists? Yet, some psychologists are interested in people, whereas others are interested in lower animals. Some are interested in basic research, whereas others are interested in applied research. Why not answer this question by enumerating some specifics?

_____

_____

_____

_____

_____

_____

_____

_____

_____

_____

_____

_____

_____

_____

_____

_____

_____

_____

_____

_____

_____

PSYCHOLOGY AS A SCIENCE: PSYCHOLOGY AND PERSONAL FREEDOM

EXERCISE 3: Which psychological perspectives seem to support the view that people are free to choose their own destinies? Which do not? Does it seem to you that people are free? Why or why not?

As you ponder this question, consider the kinds of influences that affect people's behavior and mental processes. Are we truly free? Can we know if we are truly free? What do various psychological perspectives suggest about humans' freedom to choose? Do some perspectives consider freedom to be an illusion? If so, how?

PSYCHOLOGY AS A SCIENCE: PSYCHOLOGY AND HUMAN DIVERSITY

EXERCISE 4: Why is human diversity a key issue in the science of psychology? In what ways does knowledge of human diversity contribute to our understanding of behavior and mental processes?

As you ponder this question, you may want to consider the kinds of human behavior that you might consider basic to people—that is, found in everyone in one way or another. How might the study of diversity be able to help inform us as to what is or is not basic human behavior? What are some of the other reasons for studying human diversity?

_____

_____

_____

_____

_____

_____

_____

_____

_____

_____

_____

_____

_____

_____

_____

_____

_____

_____

_____

PSYCHOLOGY AS A SCIENCE: CORRELATION VERSUS CAUSE AND EFFECT

EXERCISE 5: We can demonstrate that people who exercise are healthier than people who do not. Does this relationship prove that exercise is a causal factor in good health? Why or why not?

This exercise assesses your understanding of the role of the *selection factor* in interpreting research findings. What is the selection factor? If reference to the selection factor challenges the validity of research into the connection between exercise and health, should we conclude that exercise does *not* promote good health? Why or why not?

_____

_____

_____

_____

_____

_____

_____

_____

_____

_____

_____

_____

_____

_____

_____

_____

_____

_____

_____

_____

PSYCHOLOGY AS A SCIENCE: CORRELATION VERSUS CAUSE AND EFFECT

EXERCISE 6: Couples who live together before getting married are more likely to get divorced once they are married than couples who do not first live together. Does this research finding mean that living together before getting married causes marital instability? Why or why not? Can you think of rival explanations for the connection between living together and marital instability?

This exercise stimulates you to think about correlation versus cause and effect as well as the concept of the *rival explanation* for a correlation between two variables. What is meant by the term *rival explanation*? What factor or factors could account for *both* living together and getting divorced? Hint: One explanation might involve *attitudes* toward marriage. What type of study would you have to run to demonstrate that cohabitation prior to marriage affects the likelihood of eventual divorce? Can such a study be run? Why or why not?

_____

_____

_____

_____

_____

_____

_____

_____

_____

_____

_____

_____

_____

_____

_____

_____

_____

PSYCHOLOGY AS A SCIENCE: ETHICS

EXERCISE 7: Do you believe that it is ethical to harm lower animals in conducting research when the results may be beneficial to people? Why or why not? Do you think that there are limits to the amount of harm to which animals should be exposed? What are they?

Consider some studies that could not have been carried out without deceiving humans as to their purposes and methods. Is it ethical to deceive participants as to the purposes and methods of the research? What is meant by the principle of informed consent? Is deception of participants consistent or inconsistent with this principle?

In your response, try to consider the value of some of the studies in which participants have been deceived. Is it possible to weigh or balance the value of the research findings against the harm—or potential harm—done by the use of deception?

_____

_____

_____

_____

_____

_____

_____

_____

_____

_____

_____

_____

_____

_____

_____

_____

_____

_____

_____

_____

_____

BIOLOGY AND BEHAVIOR: WHY DO PSYCHOLOGISTS STUDY BIOLOGY?

EXERCISE 8: Because psychology is usually defined as the study of behavior and mental processes, why are psychologists interested in biological matters such as the nervous system, the endocrine system, and genetics?

Can knowledge of the brain and other parts of the nervous system enhance our understanding of behavior and mental processes? If so, how? What are the connections between the endocrine system and emotional experience? Do any behavior patterns and mental abilities seem linked to heredity? If so, what kinds of behaviors?

_____

_____

_____

_____

_____

_____

_____

_____

_____

_____

_____

_____

_____

_____

_____

_____

_____

_____

_____

_____

BIOLOGY AND BEHAVIOR: THE BIOCHEMISTRY OF PSYCHOLOGICAL PROCESSES

EXERCISE 9: Agree or disagree with the following statement and support your answer: "For every psychological event, such as a mental image or a thought, there are countless biochemical events that take place in the body."

The accuracy of this statement depends on the connections between mental processes and biochemical events, such as those that involve neural transmission of messages in the brain. What do you know about the connections between these psychological and biochemical events? Do you think that mental processes can occur in the absence of these biochemical events? Why or why not?

BIOLOGY AND BEHAVIOR: FEAR AND INDIGESTION

EXERCISE 10: Have you ever lost your appetite, been unable to eat, or thrown up because of anxiety or fear? What biological processes may have led fear to cause indigestion? (Hint: Try to answer this question in terms of the functioning of the branches or divisions of the autonomic nervous system.)

This question will also help you to understand why psychologists are interested in the functioning of the autonomic nervous system.

_____

_____

_____

_____

_____

_____

_____

_____

_____

_____

_____

_____

_____

_____

_____

_____

_____

_____

_____

_____

_____

_____

_____

BIOLOGY AND BEHAVIOR: THE ENDOCRINE SYSTEM

EXERCISE 11: Why do you think that psychologists are particularly interested in adrenaline (epinephrine) and noradrenaline (norepinephrine)?

In your answer, consider the effects of these hormones on people's feelings (emotional reactions) and behavior.

This question will also help you to understand why psychologists are interested in the functioning of the endocrine system.

BIOLOGY AND BEHAVIOR: HEREDITY

EXERCISE 12: Which family members are similar to you physically or psychologically? Which are very different? To what do you attribute the similarities and differences? Why?

In your answer, you may want to consider the effects of both nature (heredity) and nurture (environmental influences).

This question will also help you to understand why psychologists are interested in genetics and behavior genetics.

_____

_____

_____

_____

_____

_____

_____

_____

_____

_____

_____

_____

_____

_____

_____

_____

_____

_____

_____

_____

BIOLOGY AND BEHAVIOR: EVOLUTION

EXERCISE 13: According to Darwin, various species and individuals compete for the same territories, and thus organisms that are better adapted to their environments are more likely to survive (i.e., to be "naturally selected"), reproduce, and transmit their features or traits to the next generation. Which features or traits do you believe are most critical to human survival? Why?

When you think of different kinds of animals, do traits such as strength, fleetness of foot (wing or fin), and aggressiveness or social dominance come to mind? What about traits such as keen senses of vision, hearing, smell, and so on? What about intelligence, loyalty, love, and other psychological traits? Which traits seem most important to human survival? Why? Do you think that people may possess these traits as a result of evolution? Why or why not?

_____

_____

_____

_____

_____

_____

_____

_____

_____

_____

_____

_____

_____

_____

_____

_____

_____

_____

_____

DEVELOPMENTAL PSYCHOLOGY: THE NEWBORN CHILD

EXERCISE 14: Agree or disagree with the following statement and support your answer: "The newborn baby must sense the world as 'one great booming, buzzing confusion.'"

This statement was made by William James, who was a nineteenth-century authority figure in psychology. However, how do critical thinkers respond to appeals to authority? Your task here is to review what is known about the perceptual abilities of the newborn and to consider whether these abilities are likely to give rise to "one great booming, buzzing confusion." Would you attribute the newborn's perceptual abilities to nature or nurture? Why?

_____

_____

_____

_____

_____

_____

_____

_____

_____

_____

_____

_____

_____

_____

_____

_____

_____

_____

_____

_____

_____

DEVELOPMENTAL PSYCHOLOGY: PARENTING STYLES

EXERCISE 15: Would you characterize the parent figures in your life as having been authoritative, authoritarian, or permissive? How did the parenting style you experienced affect your feelings and behavior?

Try to evaluate your home experiences as objectively as possible. Does your effort to connect your experiences to your current feelings and behavior seem to be a scientific or a speculative endeavor? Explain. Do your conclusions appear to coincide with research results on dimensions of child rearing? How or how not?

_____

_____

_____

_____

_____

_____

_____

_____

_____

_____

_____

_____

_____

_____

_____

_____

_____

_____

_____

_____

_____

_____

_____

DEVELOPMENTAL PSYCHOLOGY: ASSIMILATION AND ACCOMMODATION

EXERCISE 16: Piaget's concepts of assimilation and accommodation are difficult for many students to understand. Can you provide some examples of using these mental processes in your own life, perhaps in your learning about the various areas of psychology?

The concepts of assimilation and accommodation do not apply only to children. Consider the definitions of the terms. Then find examples of how these concepts describe some aspects of your learning about psychology and, perhaps, other academic subjects. As a matter of fact, don't you engage in assimilation and accommodation every day of your life?

_____

_____

_____

_____

_____

_____

_____

_____

_____

_____

_____

_____

_____

_____

_____

_____

_____

_____

_____

_____

_____

DEVELOPMENTAL PSYCHOLOGY: MORAL REASONING

EXERCISE 17: Agree or disagree with the following statement and support your answer: "Postconventional moral judgments can actually encourage immoral behavior."

Kohlberg's views have been misunderstood on many grounds. For example, some critics argue that postconventional reasoning can lead people to break the law, which they see as immoral. Do postconventional moral judgments now and then encourage individuals to take the law into their own hands? Can you think of historical circumstances in which people have taken the law into their own hands because of postconventional moral reasoning? (Hint: You may want to consider the American Revolution, civil rights demonstrations, and so on.) Is taking the law into one's own hands always a bad thing? Why or why not?

_____

_____

_____

_____

_____

_____

_____

_____

_____

_____

_____

_____

_____

_____

_____

_____

_____

_____

_____

DEVELOPMENTAL PSYCHOLOGY: ADOLESCENCE

EXERCISE 18: G. Stanley Hall said that adolescence was a time of *sturm und drang* ("storm and stress"). Does this stereotype describe your own experiences as an adolescent? How or how not?

G. Stanley Hall assumed that the conflicts and distress of adolescence were universal and attributed them to biological changes, in which case we might expect typical adolescent behavior patterns, such as mood swings. Are your own experiences consistent with Hall's view? How or how not?

_____

_____

_____

_____

_____

_____

_____

_____

_____

_____

_____

_____

_____

_____

_____

_____

_____

_____

_____

_____

_____

DEVELOPMENTAL PSYCHOLOGY: ADOLESCENCE

EXERCISE 19: According to Erik Erikson, adolescence is a period of life during which people attempt to form their own identity. Consider your own adolescence or that of someone you know: What problems or issues did you or the other person encounter in terms of identity formation?

 Adolescents tend to form their identity in various areas of life. One area has to do with occupational roles. Other areas have to do with political and religious views, as well as sexual values. You may want to address one or more of these areas in your answer.

_____

_____

_____

_____

_____

_____

_____

_____

_____

_____

_____

_____

_____

_____

_____

_____

_____

_____

_____

_____

_____

DEVELOPMENTAL PSYCHOLOGY: LATE ADULTHOOD

EXERCISE 20: Erik Erikson wrote that one aspect of wisdom is the ability to visualize one's role in the march of history and to accept one's own death. Do you believe that acceptance of death is a sign of wisdom? (Or do you believe that wisdom means being able to accept one's own death?) Why or why not?

What is your own view of death? What is the definition of the word *wisdom*? Is it your experience that people who are "wise" calmly accept their own deaths? Is the person who makes every effort to remain alive unwise?

What is your own opinion? Erikson is somewhat of an authority figure in the field of psychology. Should that fact color your response to this question? Why or why not?

_____

_____

_____

_____

_____

_____

_____

_____

_____

_____

_____

_____

_____

_____

_____

_____

_____

_____

_____

_____

DEVELOPMENTAL PSYCHOLOGY: THE NATURE–NURTURE CONTROVERSY

EXERCISE 21: One of the great debates in psychology is the nature–nurture controversy—that is, whether nature (heredity) or nurture (environmental influences) has a greater effect on various aspects of development. Select an aspect of development, such as motor, language, or social development, and indicate whether nature or nurture has a greater influence. Support your answer.

In the case of language development, it seems to be obvious that natural human language ability is required for the understanding and production of speech. But children also learn the languages that are spoken in their environments. Is there a way to determine whether nature or nurture is the more influential aspect of language development? What about other aspects of development, such as "learning" to walk and the development of attachment to one's caregivers?

_____

_____

_____

_____

_____

_____

_____

_____

_____

_____

_____

_____

_____

_____

_____

_____

_____

_____

_____

SENSATION AND PERCEPTION: SIGNAL DETECTION

EXERCISE 22: Have you ever become so involved in doing something that you did not notice the heat or the cold? Have you gotten so used to sounds, such as those made by crickets or trains at night, that you do not perceive them anymore? How do these experiences relate to signal detection theory?

What are the effects of attention and motivation on perception? What insights are offered by signal-detection theory? By principles of adaptation?

_____

_____

_____

_____

_____

_____

_____

_____

_____

_____

_____

_____

_____

_____

_____

_____

_____

_____

_____

_____

SENSATION AND PERCEPTION: SENSORY ADAPTATION

EXERCISE 23: Have you had the experience of entering a dark theater and then seeing increasingly more light as your eyes adjust? What processes account for the adjustment? Do you first see the outlines of shapes or their colors? Why?

Refer to principles of sensory adaptation in your answer. (Hint: Black-and-white vision allows us to perceive the outlines of shapes.)

_____

_____

_____

_____

_____

_____

_____

_____

_____

_____

_____

_____

_____

_____

_____

_____

_____

_____

_____

_____

_____

_____

_____

SENSATION AND PERCEPTION: PERCEPTUAL ORGANIZATION

EXERCISE 24: Have you ever seen two people walking next to one another and then been surprised to see them split up without saying anything to one another? How do you account for the assumption that they knew one another?

    (Hint: You may want to frame your answer in terms of Gestalt principles of perceptual organization.)

_____

_____

_____

_____

_____

_____

_____

_____

_____

_____

_____

_____

_____

_____

_____

_____

_____

_____

_____

_____

_____

_____

_____

SENSATION AND PERCEPTION: PERCEPTION OF MOTION

EXERCISE 25: Have you had the experience of being in a train and not knowing whether your train or one on the next track was moving? How do you explain your confusion?

What are the different ways in which people perceive motion? Consider that the visual perception of movement is based on change of position relative to other objects.

_____

_____

_____

_____

_____

_____

_____

_____

_____

_____

_____

_____

_____

_____

_____

_____

_____

_____

_____

_____

SENSATION AND PERCEPTION: HEARING

EXERCISE 26: Are you familiar with the violin, viola, cello, and bass fiddle? How do their sounds differ? How do you account for the differences?

The two psychological dimensions of sound are pitch and loudness. Which of these two is more important in determining the difference in the sounds produced by these string instruments? Can you relate the difference in their sounds to the length of their strings?

_____

_____

_____

_____

_____

_____

_____

_____

_____

_____

_____

_____

_____

_____

_____

_____

_____

_____

_____

_____

_____

_____

_____

SENSATION AND PERCEPTION: SMELL AND TASTE

EXERCISE 27: Has food ever lost its flavor when you had a cold or an allergy attack? How do you account for the experience?

    As you consider this question, reflect on your memories of what you experienced during the cold or allergy attack. You may want to relate your thinking to the connections between the senses of smell and taste. Also consider what is meant by the *flavor* of a food.

_____

_____

_____

_____

_____

_____

_____

_____

_____

_____

_____

_____

_____

_____

_____

_____

_____

_____

_____

_____

_____

_____

_____

SENSATION AND PERCEPTION: PAIN

EXERCISE 28: Agree or disagree with the following statement and support your answer: "The best way to cope with pain is to ignore it."

What happens within the body when we are assaulted by painful stimuli? How do our attitudes toward pain exacerbate or limit pain? What are some of the ways in which psychologists help people to cope with pain? Do their methods for coping with pain differ from medical methods for doing so? If so, how? (Hint: Consider methods of *distraction* from pain.)

_____

_____

_____

_____

_____

_____

_____

_____

_____

_____

_____

_____

_____

_____

_____

_____

_____

_____

_____

_____

_____

CONSCIOUSNESS: SLEEP

EXERCISE 29: How much sleep do you need? (How do you know?) How much sleep do you get? Did you ever "pull" an all-nighter? What were the effects?

   In your answer, be critical of the nature of your evidence. How do you evaluate the adequacy of your personal "research"?

_____

_____

_____

_____

_____

_____

_____

_____

_____

_____

_____

_____

_____

_____

_____

_____

_____

_____

_____

_____

_____

_____

_____

CONSCIOUSNESS: INSOMNIA

EXERCISE 30: Do you ever have insomnia (i.e., difficulty falling asleep or remaining asleep)? Does insomnia seem to come and go with you, or does it seem to come on under particular circumstances? What do you do about it?

Here are some thoughts to consider. Many people are more likely to experience insomnia when they are undergoing periods of stress. Some people make their insomnia worse by worrying about whether they will get to sleep. Do either of these conditions seem to apply to you?

_____

_____

_____

_____

_____

_____

_____

_____

_____

_____

_____

_____

_____

_____

_____

_____

_____

_____

_____

_____

_____

CONSCIOUSNESS: SLEEP AND DREAMS

EXERCISE 31: What types of things do you dream about? Is the "stuff" of your dreams consistent with the theories of dreams discussed in your textbook?

For example, do you have the feeling that you tend to act out forbidden impulses in your dreams? Are your dreams rather mundane? What does the content of your own dreams suggest about the accuracy of the theories of dreams discussed in your textbook? How do you evaluate the adequacy of your personal "research" into dreams?

_____

_____

_____

_____

_____

_____

_____

_____

_____

_____

_____

_____

_____

_____

_____

_____

_____

_____

_____

_____

CONSCIOUSNESS: SLEEP AND HYPNOSIS

EXERCISE 32: People who are being hypnotized may be told that they are going to sleep. Are they actually going to sleep? How do you explain the effectiveness of these instructions?

What are the similarities and the differences between the states of sleep and the hypnotic "trance"? How do the expectations of the person being hypnotized play a role in hypnosis? How do people acquire these expectations?

_____

_____

_____

_____

_____

_____

_____

_____

_____

_____

_____

_____

_____

_____

_____

_____

_____

_____

_____

_____

_____

_____

_____

CONSCIOUSNESS: HYPNOTISM

EXERCISE 33: Agree or disagree with the following statement and support your answer: "You can only be hypnotized if you want to be hypnotized."

How are people hypnotized? How does the person being hypnotized participate in the process? Can you imagine someone who does not want to be hypnotized following these instructions? Is it possible to fool a person as to what is taking place and thus hypnotize him or her?

_____

_____

_____

_____

_____

_____

_____

_____

_____

_____

_____

_____

_____

_____

_____

_____

_____

_____

_____

_____

_____

_____

CONSCIOUSNESS: MEDITATION

EXERCISE 34: Agree or disagree with the following statement and support your answer: "Through meditation, people have been able to transcend the boundaries of everyday experience."

The statement, as written, may be suggestive of many kinds of spiritual or special experience. In your answer, however, define or delimit terms such as *transcend* and *everyday experience*. The nature of your answer, and the strength of your arguments, will surely depend on the definitions you use. If you do want to delve into transcendental experiences in the sense of spiritual experiences, it will probably be advisable to discuss the nature and limits of the kinds of psychological research that can address such issues. The concept of *transcending everyday experience* can also be understood in terms of doing things that enable us to overcome daily anxieties and tensions.

_____

_____

_____

_____

_____

_____

_____

_____

_____

_____

_____

_____

_____

_____

_____

_____

_____

_____

_____

_____

_____

_____

_____

CONSCIOUSNESS: BIOFEEDBACK TRAINING

EXERCISE 35: Agree or disagree with the following statement and support your answer: "Research into biofeedback training has altered the traditional distinction between *voluntary* and *involuntary* body functions."

What *is* the traditional distinction between voluntary and involuntary body functions? (Hint: You may want to refer to various branches or divisions of the nervous system, such as the autonomic nervous system, as you contemplate your answer.) Definitions are important in thinking about this issue. For example, you can raise your heart rate by running around a track.

If you decide to raise your heart rate by exercising, are you *"voluntarily"* raising your heart rate? Or, within the science of psychology, does *voluntary* behavior refer in more limited fashion to directly willed behavior? If so, does research show that people given biofeedback training can learn to directly will their hearts to accelerate or decelerate?

_____

_____

_____

_____

_____

_____

_____

_____

_____

_____

_____

_____

_____

_____

_____

_____

_____

_____

CONSCIOUSNESS: SUBSTANCE USE AND ABUSE

EXERCISE 36: Agree or disagree with the following statement and support your answer: "Cocaine and narcotics such as heroin are the most dangerous psychoactive drugs."

Note the use of the word *psychoactive* in the statement; cocaine and narcotics are only being compared with other drugs that might be used to alter consciousness or, perhaps, induce feelings of euphoria or relaxation—*not* to poisons such as curare. Nevertheless, your answer is likely to depend on which drugs you think of (do not forget alcohol and nicotine!) and on your definition of the word *dangerous*. As you think about this issue, will you use *dangerous* to mean physically dangerous ounce for ounce? Will you use *dangerous* to mean detrimental to the health of the user or to society at large? Will you be thinking in terms of one overdose, or will you be thinking in terms of the total cost to society of the drugs in question? Should you, for example, be considering fatal, alcohol-related auto accidents?

_____

_____

_____

_____

_____

_____

_____

_____

_____

_____

_____

_____

_____

_____

_____

_____

_____

_____

_____

CONSCIOUSNESS: EFFECTS OF ALCOHOL

EXERCISE 37: Agree or disagree with the following statement and support your answer: "People cannot be held responsible for their behavior when they have been drinking."

Many people misbehave when they have been drinking alcohol and then say "Don't blame me. It was the alcohol." Should they be blamed? In your answer, consider the effects of alcohol on cognition and behavior. What does the concept of "responsibility" mean? What are the roles of alcohol itself and of drinkers' expectations about alcohol's effects?

(Hint: Even if a person were to regularly lose control over his or her behavior when drinking, wouldn't he or she be responsible for choosing to drink?)

You may also consider this issue from another angle: What are the social implications of accepting the statement as written?

_____

_____

_____

_____

_____

_____

_____

_____

_____

_____

_____

_____

_____

_____

_____

_____

_____

_____

_____

_____

_____

LEARNING: CONDITIONING

EXERCISE 38: Have you heard the expression, "That rings a bell"? To what events in the history of the psychology of learning does the expression refer?

_____

_____

_____

_____

_____

_____

_____

_____

_____

_____

_____

_____

_____

_____

_____

_____

_____

_____

_____

_____

_____

_____

_____

_____

LEARNING: EXTINCTION

EXERCISE 39: What is the difference between *extinction* and *forgetting*?

How would you define each of these terms? Under what circumstances does behavior become extinguished? Under what circumstances do people forget things? Are the circumstances similar? (Hint: Extinction is a process of learning.) Is forgetting also a process of learning?

_____

_____

_____

_____

_____

_____

_____

_____

_____

_____

_____

_____

_____

_____

_____

_____

_____

_____

_____

_____

_____

_____

_____

_____

LEARNING: CONDITIONING AND COMPLEX HUMAN BEHAVIOR

EXERCISE 40: Agree or disagree with the following statement and support your answer: "Even complex human behavior can be explained as the summation of so many instances of conditioning."

Do you see the complexity and richness of human behavior as basically similar to that of lower animals? If so, you may tend to agree with the statement. Do you see human behavior as essentially different from that of lower animals? If so, you may be more likely to disagree.

Do you believe that human behavior involves cognitive maps, insights, and self-direction? If so, can these aspects of human psychology be explained in terms of the summation of so many instances of conditioning?

_____

_____

_____

_____

_____

_____

_____

_____

_____

_____

_____

_____

_____

_____

_____

_____

_____

_____

_____

_____

_____

LEARNING: LEARNING OF VISUAL-MOTOR SKILLS

EXERCISE 41: Pianists' fingers "fly" over the keys faster than they can read notes or even think notes. What kinds of learning are at work in learning to play the piano or in learning to perfectly execute a piece of music with rapid notes?

Piano playing (and music appreciation) are certainly examples of behaviors and mental processes that differentiate people from lower organisms. Is there, however, a role for simpler learning—for conditioning—in explaining the ability to play the piano and other instruments? Can the playing of one note come to serve as the stimulus for playing the second? Is there a role for cognitive learning? (For example, for deciding to learn to play the piece? For planning to practice? For deciding on a method of attack?)

_____

_____

_____

_____

_____

_____

_____

_____

_____

_____

_____

_____

_____

_____

_____

_____

_____

_____

_____

_____

LEARNING: THE ROLE OF HABIT

EXERCISE 42: William James wrote that habit is the great "flywheel" of society—that is, habit keeps society functioning. Do you agree? What role does habit play in your own life? Do you have "good habits" and "bad habits"? What are they? How did they develop? What maintains them?

_____
_____
_____
_____
_____
_____
_____
_____
_____
_____
_____
_____
_____
_____
_____
_____
_____
_____
_____
_____
_____

LEARNING: COGNITIVE ASPECTS OF LEARNING

EXERCISE 43: Have you ever studied an atlas, a road map, a cookbook, or a computer manual for "the pleasure of doing so"? In what kind of learning were you engaging? Was your behavior reinforced? If so, in what way? Did your method of learning differ from conditioning? If so, in what way?

_____

_____

_____

_____

_____

_____

_____

_____

_____

_____

_____

_____

_____

_____

_____

_____

_____

_____

_____

_____

_____

_____

LEARNING: OBSERVATIONAL LEARNING OF AGGRESSIVE BEHAVIOR

EXERCISE 44: How much violence do people in the United States and Canada today witness on television, in films, and in the streets? How does media violence affect their behavior?

In your answer, you may want to consider the results of research into the connections between watching violence on television and behaving violently as a result. You may also want to consider how violence in the media affects viewers' attitudes toward violence. Why do some people imitate the violence they see in the media, whereas other people do not?

_____

_____

_____

_____

_____

_____

_____

_____

_____

_____

_____

_____

_____

_____

_____

_____

_____

_____

_____

_____

_____

MEMORY: KINDS OF MEMORY

EXERCISE 45: What kinds of procedural memories (also called *skill memories*) do you have?

Examples of procedural memories include remembering how to hold a pen or pencil, type on a keyboard, and drive a car. Can you provide other examples? How did you acquire these procedural memories? Why do you think that they are so deeply ingrained?

_____

_____

_____

_____

_____

_____

_____

_____

_____

_____

_____

_____

_____

_____

_____

_____

_____

_____

_____

_____

_____

_____

_____

MEMORY: KINDS OF CODING OR REHEARSAL

EXERCISE 46: How do you remember how to spell the words *receive* and *weird*?

Is your ability to remember how to spell these words simply a matter of rote memorization, or do you use some sort of elaborate encoding method to help you *retrieve* the proper spelling? If so, what method(s) do you use?

_____

_____

_____

_____

_____

_____

_____

_____

_____

_____

_____

_____

_____

_____

_____

_____

_____

_____

_____

_____

_____

MEMORY: KINDS OF CODING OR REHEARSAL

EXERCISE 47: How do you try to remember names and phone numbers?

Imagine that you are meeting some attractive new people at a party. How would you normally go about remembering their names and telephone numbers? Can you think of a better way to remember them?

_____

_____

_____

_____

_____

_____

_____

_____

_____

_____

_____

_____

_____

_____

_____

_____

_____

_____

_____

_____

_____

_____

_____

MEMORY: EARLY MEMORIES

EXERCISE 48: What are your earliest memories? Are you sure? Why could these memories be distorted?

    In thinking about this question, you may want to remember the literature on infantile amnesia—why children tend not to recall events that occurred during the first couple of years of life. You may also want to refer to the literature on reconstructive memory—that is, the tendency to distort memories according to our schemas and biases.

_____

_____

_____

_____

_____

_____

_____

_____

_____

_____

_____

_____

_____

_____

_____

_____

_____

_____

_____

_____

_____

_____

_____

MEMORY: THE "QUALITY" OF MEMORY

EXERCISE 49: Do you know people with excellent memories? How about people with poor memories? How would you have explained why some people have good memories and others have poor memories before you began to study psychology? How has your study of psychology affected the ways in which you would account for a good memory or a poor memory?

You may consider many issues in answering this question. Here are two of them: The first issue involves strategies that we use to remember things. The second issue involves the biology of memory.

_____

_____

_____

_____

_____

_____

_____

_____

_____

_____

_____

_____

_____

_____

_____

_____

_____

_____

_____

_____

_____

_____

MEMORY: FORGETTING

EXERCISE 50: Are there some things that you are sure you will never forget? Why is that so?

What topics covered in your textbook seem to address this question? One is flashbulb memory. Another is the nature of long-term memory. Can you think of any others? Do you have other ideas based on your own experiences? What are they?

_____

_____

_____

_____

_____

_____

_____

_____

_____

_____

_____

_____

_____

_____

_____

_____

_____

_____

_____

_____

_____

_____

THINKING: CONCEPT FORMATION

EXERCISE 51: When you were a child, some people were probably introduced to you as Aunt Bea or Uncle Harry. Do you remember when you first understood the concept of aunt or uncle? Can you think of ways to teach these concepts to small children without using verbal explanation?

_____

_____

_____

_____

_____

_____

_____

_____

_____

_____

_____

_____

_____

_____

_____

_____

_____

_____

_____

_____

_____

_____

_____

THINKING: PROBLEM SOLVING

EXERCISE 52: How can you use subgoals to develop a strategy for doing well in this course? How about for doing well in an athletic event?

_____

_____

_____

_____

_____

_____

_____

_____

_____

_____

_____

_____

_____

_____

_____

_____

_____

_____

_____

_____

_____

_____

THINKING: CREATIVITY AND INTELLIGENCE

EXERCISE 53: In your own experience, what are the connections between creativity and intelligence? Do you know people who are highly creative in art or some other area but who do not impress you as being more intelligent overall than the average person? How do you account for their special talents?

_____

_____

_____

_____

_____

_____

_____

_____

_____

_____

_____

_____

_____

_____

_____

_____

_____

_____

_____

_____

_____

_____

THINKING: REASONING

EXERCISE 54: Do you recognize the following kind of argument?

1. John says that too much money is spent on education.
2. Is John a teacher, father, man, doctor, minister, congressional representative, or talk show host? Pick one.
3. Therefore, too much money is spent on education.

What sort of appeal is used in this argument? Is the argument logical? Is the conclusion correct? Can you think of examples of similar kinds of arguments from your own experiences?

_____

_____

_____

_____

_____

_____

_____

_____

_____

_____

_____

_____

_____

_____

_____

_____

_____

_____

_____

_____

THINKING: JUDGMENT AND DECISION MAKING

EXERCISE 55: Have you ever known people who have refused to change their minds even though they were shown to be wrong? How do you explain their reluctance to change?

Why do people tend to be overconfident in their judgments, even when they are wrong? Which reasons may apply to the behavior of people that you have witnessed?

_____

_____

_____

_____

_____

_____

_____

_____

_____

_____

_____

_____

_____

_____

_____

_____

_____

_____

_____

_____

_____

LANGUAGE DEVELOPMENT

EXERCISE 56: Can you recall any of your own experiences in learning the language spoken in your home? Do you recall any "cute" errors that you once made in your choice of words or in pronunciation?

Children tend to make a number of "charming" errors because of events such as overregularization or irregular verbs. Have you noticed such errors in the language development of younger siblings or children in your neighborhood? How do you explain them?

_____

_____

_____

_____

_____

_____

_____

_____

_____

_____

_____

_____

_____

_____

_____

_____

_____

_____

_____

_____

_____

_____

INTELLIGENCE: DEFINITION

EXERCISE 57: How would you have defined *intelligence* before you began this course? How do psychologists' definitions of intelligence agree with, or differ from, your own? How would you compare your definition with those about which you have read?

_____

_____

_____

_____

_____

_____

_____

_____

_____

_____

_____

_____

_____

_____

_____

_____

_____

_____

_____

_____

_____

_____

_____

INTELLIGENCE: INTELLIGENCE TESTING

EXERCISE 58: Have you ever taken an intelligence test? Was it an individual test or a group test? What was the experience like? Were you informed as to how well you did on the test? Do you believe that the test assessed you fairly or arrived at an accurate estimate of your intelligence?

You may have taken such tests as early as in primary school. They may have been group or individual tests. You may or may not have been informed about the purpose of the testing.

Were you or your family ever informed of the results of the test? Why or why not? If you were not informed, do you think that you should have been informed? Why or why not?

_____

_____

_____

_____

_____

_____

_____

_____

_____

_____

_____

_____

_____

_____

_____

_____

_____

_____

_____

_____

_____

INTELLIGENCE: INDIVIDUAL AND SOCIOCULTURAL DIFFERENCES IN INTELLIGENCE

EXERCISE 59: Lower-class children in the United States obtain IQ scores approximately 10 to 15 points lower than those obtained by middle- and upper-class children. Explain this finding from a genetic point of view. Then explain it from an environmental point of view. Are you more sympathetic toward one of these views than the other? If so, why?

INTELLIGENCE: INTELLIGENCE AND THE HOME ENVIRONMENT

EXERCISE 60: As you reflect on your own childhood, can you point to any kinds of family or educational experiences that seem to have had an impact on your intellectual development? Would you say that your background, overall, was deprived or enriched? In what ways?

In your answer, you may want to refer to the kinds of factors in the home that have been shown to be connected with intellectual development.

_____

_____

_____

_____

_____

_____

_____

_____

_____

_____

_____

_____

_____

_____

_____

_____

_____

_____

_____

_____

_____

_____

_____

MOTIVATION: INSTINCTS

EXERCISE 61: The behavior of many organisms is motivated by instincts. What are instincts? Do you believe that people have instincts? What kinds of instincts? What is your evidence for your belief?

What kinds of research methods have been used to try to determine whether behavior is instinctive or learned. Has such research been conducted with humans? Why or why not?

_____

_____

_____

_____

_____

_____

_____

_____

_____

_____

_____

_____

_____

_____

_____

_____

_____

_____

_____

_____

_____

MOTIVATION: THE HIERARCHY OF NEEDS

EXERCISE 62: Abraham Maslow constructed a hierarchy of needs that he believed governed human behavior. What needs in his hierarchy are you attempting to meet by attending college? Explain how.

_____

_____

_____

_____

_____

_____

_____

_____

_____

_____

_____

_____

_____

_____

_____

_____

_____

_____

_____

_____

_____

_____

MOTIVATION: HUNGER

EXERCISE 63: People eat for many reasons. The hunger drive is one of them. Do you eat only when you are hungry or also for other reasons? If so, what are the other reasons?

This question aims to help you understand the various factors that contribute to eating behavior in humans. Reflect on occasions when you have eaten when not hungry—perhaps on an occasion or two when you have eaten something even when you were full. What are the implications of such behavior for maintaining a healthful weight?

_____

_____

_____

_____

_____

_____

_____

_____

_____

_____

_____

_____

_____

_____

_____

_____

_____

_____

_____

_____

_____

MOTIVATION: HUNGER

EXERCISE 64: Agree or disagree with the following statement and support your answer: "People who are overweight simply eat too much."

This statement reflects a widely held view that overweight people cannot or—perhaps more to the point—*will not* control what they eat and therefore they eat too much. The statement, similar to many other kinds of common sense (or common nonsense) is an overgeneralization. It also has a moralistic ring.

However, critical thinkers avoid overgeneralizations.

What factors are shown by psychological research to be involved in obesity? Do they *all* involve eating too much? (What, by the way, does "too much" mean?) Do some people, for example, find it difficult to lose weight even when they consume fewer calories than weight charts recommend to maintain their weights?

_____

_____

_____

_____

_____

_____

_____

_____

_____

_____

_____

_____

_____

_____

_____

_____

_____

_____

_____

_____

_____

MOTIVATION: IS THERE A NEED FOR STIMULATION?

EXERCISE 65: Do you find it relaxing to lie on the beach and "do nothing"? For how long? Or do you find it difficult to lie on the beach and do nothing? Why?

You may want to frame your answer in terms of your perceived needs for stimulation and activity. What do you think are the origins of these needs in yourself? Why?

_____

_____

_____

_____

_____

_____

_____

_____

_____

_____

_____

_____

_____

_____

_____

_____

_____

_____

_____

_____

_____

_____

MOTIVATION: ACHIEVEMENT MOTIVATION

EXERCISE 66: Do you want to do well in this course? How hard will you strive to do well? How would you rate your own level of achievement motivation with that of other people you know? How do you account for the differences? When you consider your own experiences in life, where does the achievement motivation (or lack of it) originate?

_____

_____

_____

_____

_____

_____

_____

_____

_____

_____

_____

_____

_____

_____

_____

_____

_____

_____

_____

_____

_____

_____

MOTIVATION: AGGRESSION

EXERCISE 67: Aggressiveness is valued in some circumstances, as in sports and in warfare, but aggression is also a serious social problem. What were your beliefs about why some people are more aggressive than others before you began this course? How has the information in this course affected your views?

You may want to frame your answer in terms of the theories of motivation that are discussed in your textbook.

Also feel free to refer to other perspectives that occur to you, such as a religious or moral perspective, or, perhaps, "common sense."

MOTIVATION: COGNITIVE-DISSONANCE THEORY

EXERCISE 68: Cognitive-dissonance theory is of interest to psychologists who study motivation because people are motivated to have their cognitions in harmony. It is also of interest to social psychologists because it concerns attitudes—a topic in social psychology. Consider the concept of *effort justification,* one aspect of cognitive-dissonance theory. Were you or someone you know subjected to rough hazing upon joining a sorority, fraternity, or club? Did the experience affect your feelings or the other person's feelings about being a member of the group? How? Can you connect the experience to cognitive-dissonance theory?

_____

_____

_____

_____

_____

_____

_____

_____

_____

_____

_____

_____

_____

_____

_____

_____

_____

_____

_____

_____

_____

EMOTION: THE NATURE OF EMOTIONS

EXERCISE 69: Do you know people who are highly emotional? What behavior leads you to infer that they are emotional?

_____

_____

_____

_____

_____

_____

_____

_____

_____

_____

_____

_____

_____

_____

_____

_____

_____

_____

_____

_____

_____

_____

_____

_____

EMOTION: THE EXPRESSION OF EMOTIONS

EXERCISE 70: When you are upset, do you tend to "keep a stiff upper lip" or to "let it all hang out"? Which do you believe is a better strategy for coping with negative feelings? Why?

_____

_____

_____

_____

_____

_____

_____

_____

_____

_____

_____

_____

_____

_____

_____

_____

_____

_____

_____

_____

_____

_____

EMOTION: THEORIES OF EMOTION

EXERCISE 71: Assume that you are trying to overcome feelings of depression. Do you think that it is a better idea to wait until you feel better before you get out and do things, or do you think that you should try to force yourself to get out and do things, regardless whether you "feel up to it"? Why?

In your answer, you may want to consider what the theories of emotion discussed in your textbook might suggest about this issue. Which of these behavior patterns, for example, would be endorsed by the James-Lange theory of emotion?

_____

_____

_____

_____

_____

_____

_____

_____

_____

_____

_____

_____

_____

_____

_____

_____

_____

_____

_____

_____

_____

EMOTION: LYING

EXERCISE 72: Despite questions about their validity, polygraph or "lie detector" tests are frequently used to help determine whether people are telling the truth. How about you? What do you look for in an effort to determine whether someone is lying to you? What clues do you seek? Can you "keep a straight face" when you lie?

You may want to consider the role of body language in our conclusions as to whether someone is lying to us or telling us the truth? What about stereotypes such as "shifty eyes"?

_____

_____

_____

_____

_____

_____

_____

_____

_____

_____

_____

_____

_____

_____

_____

_____

_____

_____

_____

_____

_____

PERSONALITY: PSYCHODYNAMIC THEORY

EXERCISE 73: Agree or disagree with the following statement and support your answer: "People are basically antisocial. Their primitive impulses must be suppressed and repressed if they are to function productively within social settings."

This statement is consistent with traditional Freudian theory. However, critical thinkers do not accept statements solely on the basis of authority, even when that authority is Sigmund Freud. Critical thinkers also pay attention to the definitions of terms: What do the words *basically* and *antisocial* mean? What is the nature of the evidence for the statement?

_____

_____

_____

_____

_____

_____

_____

_____

_____

_____

_____

_____

_____

_____

_____

_____

_____

_____

_____

_____

_____

_____

PERSONALITY: PSYCHODYNAMIC THEORY

EXERCISE 74: If you were fixated in a stage of psychosexual development, which stage would it be? Why?

What are the stages of psychosexual development according to Freud? What characteristics or personality traits are associated with each stage?

Why did Freud believe that such traits represented fixation in a given stage of development? (What is the theoretical explanation?)

_____

_____

_____

_____

_____

_____

_____

_____

_____

_____

_____

_____

_____

_____

_____

_____

_____

_____

_____

_____

_____

_____

PERSONALITY: TRAIT THEORY

EXERCISE 75: What traits do you refer to when you are describing yourself? For example, do you see yourself as being shy or outgoing? Emotionally stable or easily upset? Conscientious or easygoing? Agreeable or stubborn? Open or closed off to new experiences?

What is the evidence for your conclusions about yourself? Where do your traits originate? Are you satisfied with your personality traits? Why or why not?

_____

_____

_____

_____

_____

_____

_____

_____

_____

_____

_____

_____

_____

_____

_____

_____

_____

_____

_____

_____

_____

PERSONALITY: PERSONALITY THEORY AND FREE WILL

EXERCISE 76: Given cultural and social conditioning, is true freedom possible? To behaviorists, telling ourselves that we have free will is determined by the environment. Is free will merely an illusion? What is the evidence for your belief?

"You have freedom when you're easy in your harness," wrote the poet Robert Frost.

The views of John B. Watson and B. F. Skinner largely discard the notions of personal freedom, choice, and self-direction. Most of us assume that our wants originate within us. But Skinner suggests that environmental influences such as parental approval and social custom shape us into *wanting* certain things and *not wanting* others. To Watson and Skinner, even telling ourselves that we have free will is determined by the environment as is our becoming startled at a sudden noise.

What is *freedom*? What is *true* freedom? (Does "true freedom" differ from "freedom," or does the phrase simply overdescribe the concept?) Is it possible that people can be shaped into telling themselves (believing) that they are free when their behavior is actually quite circumscribed within social and cultural limits? Is it possible, for example, that people in the United States are compelled to see themselves as being free to choose their own attitudes and behaviors? If so, would it be possible to see through such cultural conditioning?

_____

_____

_____

_____

_____

_____

_____

_____

_____

_____

_____

_____

_____

_____

_____

_____

PERSONALITY: SOCIAL-COGNITIVE THEORY

EXERCISE 77: Social-cognitive theorists suggest that our self-efficacy expectations are connected with how hard we work at things. (Social-cognitive theorists also suggest that psychotherapy helps people to change their outlook on life from "I can't" to "I *can*.") Do examples from your own life support this view?

_____

_____

_____

_____

_____

_____

_____

_____

_____

_____

_____

_____

_____

_____

_____

_____

_____

_____

_____

_____

_____

_____

_____

PERSONALITY: SELF THEORY

EXERCISE 78: Do you see yourself as a self-actualizer? Why or why not?

_____

_____

_____

_____

_____

_____

_____

_____

_____

_____

_____

_____

_____

_____

_____

_____

_____

_____

_____

_____

_____

_____

PERSONALITY: SELF THEORY

EXERCISE 79: According to Carl Rogers, self-esteem is an extremely important personality trait. How would you describe your own level of self-esteem? What are the effects of your self-esteem on your feelings about yourself and the world around you?

Rogers suggested that low self-esteem derives from the failure to meet other people's conditions of worth. What are conditions of worth? What conditions of worth did you experience when you were younger? What conditions of worth are you experiencing today? How do these conditions of worth seem to have affected your own self-esteem?

_____

_____

_____

_____

_____

_____

_____

_____

_____

_____

_____

_____

_____

_____

_____

_____

_____

_____

_____

_____

_____

_____

PERSONALITY: INDIVIDUALISM VERSUS COLLECTIVISM

EXERCISE 80: Sociocultural factors, such as being reared in an individualistic or collectivist society, affect the personality development of individuals. When you were a child, were you given conflicting messages about the importance of competing successfully and of sharing? Do you believe that the experiences in your own home were more oriented toward encouraging individualism or collectivism? How so?

How are the values of competing successfully and of sharing in conflict? How are they connected with concepts of individualism and collectivism?

Does the ethnic group(s) to which you belong tend to give priority to individualism or collectivism? If so, in what ways? How have the values of your group(s) influenced you?

_____

_____

_____

_____

_____

_____

_____

_____

_____

_____

_____

_____

_____

_____

_____

_____

_____

_____

_____

_____

PERSONALITY: PERSONALITY TESTS

EXERCISE 81: Do you believe that psychological tests are of use in assessing people's rightness for various kinds of jobs or in assessing psychological problems? Why or why not?

_____

_____

_____

_____

_____

_____

_____

_____

_____

_____

_____

_____

_____

_____

_____

_____

_____

_____

_____

_____

_____

_____

_____

_____

PERSONALITY: GENDER ROLES AND STEREOTYPES

EXERCISE 82: What are the gender role stereotypes in our culture? Would you say that your own behavior patterns and psychological traits are consistent with stereotypical female or male gender roles? Have your behaviors and traits affected your self-concept? If so, how?

_____

_____

_____

_____

_____

_____

_____

_____

_____

_____

_____

_____

_____

_____

_____

_____

_____

_____

_____

_____

_____

_____

PERSONALITY: GENDER-TYPING

EXERCISE 83: Gender-typing refers to the processes by which children develop behavior patterns and mental processes that are consistent with the female or male gender role stereotypes within a culture. What theory or perspective on gender-typing best describes your own experiences with gender-typing?

According to your point of view, does gender-typing seem to be mainly a biological or psychological process? Why? Can you recall any experiences that contributed to your gender-typing?

_____

_____

_____

_____

_____

_____

_____

_____

_____

_____

_____

_____

_____

_____

_____

_____

_____

_____

_____

_____

_____

_____

_____

_____

_____

HEALTH PSYCHOLOGY: LIFE CHANGES AND DAILY HASSLES

EXERCISE 84: What kinds of life changes and daily hassles are you experiencing? Do you find these events stressful? How do you know?

_____

_____

_____

_____

_____

_____

_____

_____

_____

_____

_____

_____

_____

_____

_____

_____

_____

_____

_____

_____

_____

_____

HEALTH PSYCHOLOGY: FACTORS IN HEALTH AND ILLNESS

EXERCISE 85: Agree or disagree with the following statement and support your answer: "Health is basically a matter of heredity or luck. People cannot really do much to improve their health or stave off illness."

_____

_____

_____

_____

_____

_____

_____

_____

_____

_____

_____

_____

_____

_____

_____

_____

_____

_____

_____

_____

_____

_____

_____

_____

HEALTH PSYCHOLOGY: FACTORS IN HEALTH AND ILLNESS

EXERCISE 86: Consider your sociocultural background: What health problems are more common, or less common, among people of your background than among the U.S. population in general? Why do you think these problems are more or less common among people of your background?

_____

_____

_____

_____

_____

_____

_____

_____

_____

_____

_____

_____

_____

_____

_____

_____

_____

_____

_____

_____

_____

_____

PSYCHOLOGICAL DISORDERS: DEFINITION OF PSYCHOLOGICAL DISORDER

EXERCISE 87: When is it normal to feel anxious or depressed? When is it abnormal? How can you tell the difference? Can you think of circumstances in which it would be abnormal *not* to feel anxious or depressed?

_____

_____

_____

_____

_____

_____

_____

_____

_____

_____

_____

_____

_____

_____

_____

_____

_____

_____

_____

_____

_____

_____

PSYCHOLOGICAL DISORDERS: PHOBIAS

EXERCISE 88: Do you know anyone with a phobia? What kind of phobia? What separates this "phobia" from a run-of-the-mill "fear"? What does the person say to him- or herself (i.e., think) in the presence of the feared object or situation? What does he or she think is the origin of the phobia?

_____

_____

_____

_____

_____

_____

_____

_____

_____

_____

_____

_____

_____

_____

_____

_____

_____

_____

_____

_____

_____

_____

_____

_____

PSYCHOLOGICAL DISORDERS: PANIC DISORDER

EXERCISE 89: Do you ever find yourself "in a panic"? Under what circumstances? What is the difference between "being in a panic" and having a panic disorder?

    This exercise highlights a difference between casual use of psychological-sounding terms and accurate use of psychological terms. What do people usually mean when they say that they are "in a panic"? How does the DSM and your textbook define *panic disorder*? In what ways do the terms or phrases overlap? In what ways are they different?

_____

_____

_____

_____

_____

_____

_____

_____

_____

_____

_____

_____

_____

_____

_____

_____

_____

_____

_____

_____

_____

PSYCHOLOGICAL DISORDERS: DISSOCIATIVE AMNESIA

EXERCISE 90: Have you ever known people to claim that they had "amnesia" for some episode or event? When you read about dissociative amnesia in your textbook, do you think that the term was used correctly? Why or why not?

Similar to the previous exercise, this exercise highlights a difference between casual use of psychological-sounding terms and accurate (or professional) use of psychological terms. What do people usually mean when they say that they have "amnesia" for some event?

How does the DSM and your textbook define *dissociative amnesia*? How do the terms or phrases overlap? How are they different? (What other kinds of amnesia are discussed in your textbook? Do any of them apply to this discussion?)

_____

_____

_____

_____

_____

_____

_____

_____

_____

_____

_____

_____

_____

_____

_____

_____

_____

_____

_____

_____

PSYCHOLOGICAL DISORDERS: DEPRESSION

EXERCISE 91: Do you think that you would find it easy or difficult to admit to having feelings of depression? Why?

This exercise addresses the common stigmatization of people who admit to having psychological problems, such as feelings of depression. In your experience, do women or men find it easier to admit to having such feelings? Why?

_____

_____

_____

_____

_____

_____

_____

_____

_____

_____

_____

_____

_____

_____

_____

_____

_____

_____

_____

_____

_____

_____

_____

PSYCHOLOGICAL DISORDERS: SUICIDE

EXERCISE 92: Agree or disagree with the following statement and support your answer: "It is abnormal to consider committing suicide."

Critical thinkers pay attention to the definitions of terms and to the premises or arguments. Note, first of all, that this exercise distinguishes between considering suicide and committing suicide. Second, the various possible meanings of the word *abnormal* need to be considered. For example, abnormality can be defined in terms of statistical rareness or in terms of deviation from ideal (or idealized) behavior. Regardless of how you respond in this exercise, consider the meanings of the terms you use.

_____

_____

_____

_____

_____

_____

_____

_____

_____

_____

_____

_____

_____

_____

_____

_____

_____

_____

_____

_____

_____

_____

PSYCHOLOGICAL DISORDERS: DISSOCIATIVE IDENTITY DISORDER VERSUS SCHIZOPHRENIA

EXERCISE 93: Have you ever heard the expression "split personality"? Does the expression seem to apply more to dissociative identity disorder or schizophrenia? Why?

In your discussion, you may want to refer to the term used for dissociative identity disorder in the previous edition of the DSM—*multiple personality disorder.*

_____

_____

_____

_____

_____

_____

_____

_____

_____

_____

_____

_____

_____

_____

_____

_____

_____

_____

_____

_____

_____

_____

PSYCHOLOGICAL DISORDERS: EATING DISORDERS

EXERCISE 94: Why do you think that women are so much more likely than men to be diagnosed with the eating disorders of anorexia nervosa or bulimia nervosa?

_____

_____

_____

_____

_____

_____

_____

_____

_____

_____

_____

_____

_____

_____

_____

_____

_____

_____

_____

_____

_____

_____

METHODS OF THERAPY: PSYCHOTHERAPY VERSUS COMMON SENSE

EXERCISE 95: Agree or disagree with the following statement and support your answer: "Psychotherapy is just common sense."

This belief that psychotherapy is just common sense is perhaps a corollary of the often-heard opinion that everyone and anyone is a psychologist on the basis of life experiences. That is, can't anyone offer advice to people with psychological problems? As a psychologist, I would disagree. I would define *psychotherapy* and discuss the kinds of knowledge and training that shape psychologists into therapists. What do you think? Why?

_____

_____

_____

_____

_____

_____

_____

_____

_____

_____

_____

_____

_____

_____

_____

_____

_____

_____

_____

_____

_____

_____

METHODS OF THERAPY: BEHAVIOR THERAPY

EXERCISE 96: Can you relate the methods of behavior therapy discussed in your textbook to principles of conditioning and observational learning? For example, what about the methods that behavior therapists use to reduce fears?

_____

_____

_____

_____

_____

_____

_____

_____

_____

_____

_____

_____

_____

_____

_____

_____

_____

_____

_____

_____

_____

_____

METHODS OF THERAPY: COGNITIVE THERAPY

EXERCISE 97: Do you ever magnify the importance of negative events? If so, does this way of thinking about events ever give rise to feelings of frustration, anxiety, or depression? What can you do about it? (What do cognitive therapists do about it?)

_____

_____

_____

_____

_____

_____

_____

_____

_____

_____

_____

_____

_____

_____

_____

_____

_____

_____

_____

_____

_____

_____

METHODS OF THERAPY: COGNITIVE THERAPY

EXERCISE 98: Do you believe that you must have the love and approval of people who are important to you? If so, does this belief ever give rise to feelings of frustration, anxiety, or depression? What can you do about it? (What do cognitive therapists do about it?)

_____

_____

_____

_____

_____

_____

_____

_____

_____

_____

_____

_____

_____

_____

_____

_____

_____

_____

_____

_____

_____

_____

METHODS OF THERAPY: COGNITIVE THERAPY

EXERCISE 99: Do you believe that you must prove yourself to be thoroughly competent, adequate, and achieving? If so, does this belief ever give rise to feelings of frustration, anxiety, or depression? What can you do about it? (What do cognitive therapists do about it?)

_____

_____

_____

_____

_____

_____

_____

_____

_____

_____

_____

_____

_____

_____

_____

_____

_____

_____

_____

_____

_____

_____

_____

METHODS OF THERAPY: ASSESSMENT OF EFFICACY OF PSYCHOTHERAPY

EXERCISE 100: Justin swears that he feels much better because of psychoanalysis. Deborah swears by her experience with Gestalt therapy. Are these endorsements acceptable as scientific evidence? Why or why not?

Most of us know people who endorse certain kinds of psychotherapy, or megavitamins, or even spiritual healing. In critically thinking about the endorsements of Justin and Deborah, consider the ways in which their experiences fall short of the kinds of research methods that psychologists find to be acceptable.

_____

_____

_____

_____

_____

_____

_____

_____

_____

_____

_____

_____

_____

_____

_____

_____

_____

_____

_____

_____

_____

_____

METHODS OF THERAPY: ASSESSMENT OF EFFICACY OF PSYCHOTHERAPY

EXERCISE 101: Agree or disagree with the following statement and support your answer: "It has never been shown that psychotherapy does any good."

This statement is outdated at best. It also sounds a bit prejudiced and just plain foolish, but it is consistent with the views expressed in a paper published by Hans Eysenck in 1952. Eysenck argued that although most people who had psychotherapy showed improvement, it had not been shown that the effects of psychotherapy were superior to "spontaneous remission"—getting better, that is, simply as a function of the passage of time.

What does the evidence say about the effects of psychotherapy? Is it still possible to maintain that the effects of psychotherapy are not superior to spontaneous remission?

Note, too, that critical thinkers do not overgeneralize or, in this case, lump all forms of psychotherapy together.

_____

_____

_____

_____

_____

_____

_____

_____

_____

_____

_____

_____

_____

_____

_____

_____

_____

_____

METHODS OF THERAPY: ASSESSMENT OF EFFICACY OF PSYCHOANALYSIS

EXERCISE 102: Agree or disagree with the following statement and support your answer: "The effects of traditional psychoanalysis cannot be determined by the experimental method."

Many psychoanalysts argue that traditional psychoanalysis cannot be subjected to experimental analysis. Does this claim make sense? In arriving at your own conclusions, you may want to consider experimental research methods, including the functions of random assignment, control groups, and "blinds." Also consider the nature of traditional psychoanalysis methods and whether blinds could be used.

METHODS OF THERAPY: CHEMOTHERAPY

EXERCISE 103: Agree or disagree with the following statement and support your answer: "Drugs cause more problems than they solve when they are used to treat people with psychological disorders."

Drugs is a buzzword, that is, a loaded term (consider the "Just say no" to drugs campaign). However, drugs as a method of therapy are known more technically as chemotherapy.

In thinking critically about this statement, try to avoid overgeneralizing. Is chemotherapy, for example, of greater benefit to people with some problems than with others?

_____

_____

_____

_____

_____

_____

_____

_____

_____

_____

_____

_____

_____

_____

_____

_____

_____

_____

_____

_____

_____

_____

_____

METHODS OF THERAPY: CHEMOTHERAPY

EXERCISE 104: Agree or disagree with the following statement and support your answer: "Biological treatments only provide a sort of Band-Aid therapy for psychological disorders. They don't get at the heart of the problems."

Critical thinkers consider the meanings of the terms used in arguments. What is meant by *Band-Aid therapy?* What is meant by the *heart* of a problem? Moreover, critical thinkers avoid overgeneralization. For example, is it possible that biological treatments are more likely to get at the "heart" of some kinds of psychological disorders than others?

_____

_____

_____

_____

_____

_____

_____

_____

_____

_____

_____

_____

_____

_____

_____

_____

_____

_____

_____

_____

_____

_____

SOCIAL PSYCHOLOGY: ATTITUDES AND BEHAVIOR

EXERCISE 105: Agree or disagree with the following statement and support your answer: "People vote their consciences."

The statement sounds correct and assumes that we can predict people's behavior from knowledge of their attitudes. However, how many people actually vote? Moreover, can we always predict people's behavior from knowledge of their expressed attitudes? Even if we know of people's genuine attitudes, is their behavior always consistent with their attitudes? (Sometimes statements that sound simple are actually complex.)

SOCIAL PSYCHOLOGY: PERSUASION

EXERCISE 106: Are you entertained by radio or television commercials? Which ones? Why? Did these commercials ever convince you to buy a product? Which one? Was the commercial accurate?

This exercise asks you to record your personal experiences with commercials. Do you think that you have been persuaded by commercials? Why or why not? Do you want to think that you are not a person who can be influenced by commercials? If so, why?

_____

_____

_____

_____

_____

_____

_____

_____

_____

_____

_____

_____

_____

_____

_____

_____

_____

_____

_____

_____

_____

SOCIAL PSYCHOLOGY: FIRST IMPRESSIONS

EXERCISE 107: Think of an instance in which you tried to make a good first impression on someone. How did you do it? Why is it important to try to make a good first impression?

_____

_____

_____

_____

_____

_____

_____

_____

_____

_____

_____

_____

_____

_____

_____

_____

_____

_____

_____

_____

_____

_____

_____

SOCIAL PSYCHOLOGY: INTERPERSONAL ATTRACTION

EXERCISE 108: Agree or disagree with the following statement and support your answer: "Beauty is in the eye of the beholder."

Critical thinkers pay attention to the definitions of terms. The phrase *"in the eye of the beholder"* is poetic, but what does it mean? Does it mean that standards for physical attractiveness are subjective? Does the evidence suggest that there are no universal or widely held standards for beauty? What does the research show about the roles of attitudinal similarity and reciprocity in attraction? Do these issues bring in subjective elements? (That is, are they likely to render a person's appeal unique?) If so, how?

_____

_____

_____

_____

_____

_____

_____

_____

_____

_____

_____

_____

_____

_____

_____

_____

_____

_____

_____

_____

_____

_____

SOCIAL PSYCHOLOGY: INTERPERSONAL ATTRACTION

EXERCISE 109: Agree or disagree with the following statement and support your answer: "Opposites attract."

Here is a "truism." Are not women and men opposites, and are they not attracted to one another? (Watch out! Do not be too quick to grant me my premise that women and men are "opposites." Are they?) Are we not drawn to "forbidden fruit"? Of course, if we limit our definition of "opposites" to people of the other gender, we will be on safe ground when we claim that "Opposites attract"—at least most of the time. However, will our conclusions be the same when we critically examine this saying on the basis of attitudes?

_____

_____

_____

_____

_____

_____

_____

_____

_____

_____

_____

_____

_____

_____

_____

_____

_____

_____

_____

_____

_____

SOCIAL PSYCHOLOGY: CONFORMITY

EXERCISE 110: Can you think of some instances in which you have conformed to social pressure? (Would you wear blue jeans if everyone else wore slacks or skirts?) Have the pressures placed on you by your own sociocultural group ever come into conflict with the values and customs of the United States at large? If so, how?

_____

_____

_____

_____

_____

_____

_____

_____

_____

_____

_____

_____

_____

_____

_____

_____

_____

_____

_____

_____

_____

_____

SOCIAL PSYCHOLOGY: GROUP DECISION MAKING

EXERCISE 111: Have you ever been a member of a committee or other group decision-making body? Did the group make the decisions democratically, or did a powerful leader emerge? Were the decisions made more or less conservative than the decisions you would probably have made on your own? Why?

_____

_____

_____

_____

_____

_____

_____

_____

_____

_____

_____

_____

_____

_____

_____

_____

_____

_____

_____

_____

_____

_____

_____

SOCIAL PSYCHOLOGY: GROUP DYNAMICS

EXERCISE 112: Did you ever do something as a member of a group that you probably would not have done if you had been acting alone? What was it? Why do you think that you did it as a group member?

_____

_____

_____

_____

_____

_____

_____

_____

_____

_____

_____

_____

_____

_____

_____

_____

_____

_____

_____

_____

_____

_____

ENVIRONMENTAL PSYCHOLOGY

EXERCISE 113: As you take this course, crises loom concerning disposal of toxic wastes, industrial and vehicular emissions, population growth, devastation of the rain forest, pollution, and other environmental issues. You dwell on planet Earth. It is your home. How can you become better informed? How can you encourage people to be kinder to the environment? List some actions that you can take.

_____

_____

_____

_____

_____

_____

_____

_____

_____

_____

_____

_____

_____

_____

_____

_____

_____

_____

_____

_____

_____

_____

_____

_____

ENVIRONMENTAL PSYCHOLOGY

EXERCISE 114: Agree or disagree with the following statement and support your answer: "Crowding people together is aversive."

If you picture the statement as referring to being wedged into a subway car with perspiring commuters on a July day, it seems true enough. But let us avoid oversimplification and let us weigh all the evidence. Do our situations (our reasons for being where we are) and our attitudes have much to do with our responses to crowding?

_____

_____

_____

_____

_____

_____

_____

_____

_____

_____

_____

_____

_____

_____

_____

_____

_____

_____

_____

_____

_____